31 more great bible studies for youth

by Keith Stulp

CRC Publications
Reformed Church Press
Youth Unlimited

CRC Publications, Reformed Church Press, and Youth Unlimited thank Keith Stulp for writing this course for high school students. Stulp is a Young Life leader from Grand Rapids, Michigan.

We welcome your comments. Call us at 1-800-333-8300 or e-mail us at editors@crcpublications.org.

ISBN 1-56212-526-5

10 9 8 7 6 5 4 3 2 1

Contents

Proverbs: Great Advice for Everyday Living

Philemon: Doing the Right Thing

User's Guide

Like its popular predecessors *32 Great Bible Studies for Youth* and *29 More Great Bible Studies for Youth*, *31 More Great Bible Studies for Youth* offers photocopiable, one-page Bible studies on themes of interest to high school youth. But while the first two books were organized topically, this third book is organized around certain books of the Bible—James, Psalms, Proverbs, and Philemon—as well as the parables of Jesus. You'll find the material simple to use, complete, and biblically responsible. Using a straightforward approach, it treats high schoolers as responsible young adults who want to learn more about the Bible and its meaning for their lives. Its goal is to help them practice that Word in their daily living.

This course is readily adaptable to a variety of settings and uses. The course is available in both print and electronic format. *31 More Great Bible Studies for Youth* is a joint publication of CRC Publications, Reformed Church Press, and Youth Unlimited.

WHERE TO USE THESE STUDIES

Student-Led Groups
31 More Great Bible Studies for Youth was written especially for student-led groups of high schoolers who are conducting their own Bible study without the direct supervision of adult leaders. You'll want to read author Keith Stulp's comments on using this material for that purpose—please see pages 9-11 of this book.

Student-led Bible study groups are becoming increasingly popular in high schools, youth group meetings, retreats, and other settings. Adult leaders of such groups usually work with student leaders (of small groups), helping them select materials, plan their meetings, and handle any problems or special needs. Typically, adult leaders also convene the various small groups into large-group meetings.

If you are working with student-led groups, you'll find a handout called **Instructions for Student-Led Groups,** which you can photocopy and give to small group leaders. They, in turn, can give it to their group members, if they wish. See pages 13-14.

Student-led small groups usually work best with five to ten students in each small group.

Youth Groups

If you are looking for high-quality Bible studies for your youth group that require minimal preparation, these materials will serve you well.

Within your youth group, you might do the Warm-up questions with the whole group, then break into smaller groups for the Bible study itself, and finish by returning to the large group for the Group Talk discussion questions at the end of each study. Or, if you prefer, walk with the students through the entire study.

Each Bible study will take from thirty-five to sixty minutes, depending on how many of the questions you use and the extent of your discussion.

Retreats

Planning a retreat is a lot easier once you've selected a theme or topic on which to focus. Check out the topics of the various units in this course, then use the Bible studies from one unit—say James or Psalms—as the core of your retreat. Build your retreat around the studies, letting students run their own small group Bible studies. Supplement the studies with topic-related activities, games, guest speakers, recreational time, and so on.

Church School

High schoolers in church school settings often need a break from longer blocks of curriculum. Slip in a unit from *31 More Great* on the parables of Jesus or Proverbs. Maybe let students run all or part of their own Bible studies. Or, if it goes over well, try *31 More Great* for a semester or even longer.

FORMAT

There are 31 Bible studies from which you can choose (plus a couple of introductory meetings for getting started). The studies are clustered in units ranging from two to eight meetings each. The units cover James, Psalms, the parables of Jesus, Proverbs, and Philemon. It doesn't matter what order you take the units in, but once you and the group choose a topic, you'll probably want to take the meetings within that unit in sequence.

Each Bible study is complete on two sides of a single page. Don't feel that you have to discuss every question on these sheets. If a question bombs, drop it and move on to the next one. If a question produces some good talk, stay with it for a while. Going through all the questions will probably take your group at least forty-five minutes.

Meetings should begin with the **Warm-up** questions. Please note that although the questions are in the right-hand column, they should be read first, before the introductory comments. The first question is often just an icebreaker meant to get the group talking to each other. It may or many not have anything to do with the topic. The second and third questions should definitely nudge the group toward the theme of the meeting.

After the warm-up questions, have group members take turns reading the **introductory comments** in the left-hand column. The comments are meant to introduce the topic and the Bible study on side 2.

On side 2 you'll find **Scripture** and six related **questions.** Before reading Scripture, have someone read question 1—it will give the group something to look for while reading. Questions 1-3 get at important facts in the passage. Questions 4-6 interpret and apply the passage. Question 6 is especially important because it asks teens to personalize the Bible study and to practice (during the week) what they learned. Author Keith Stulp says, "I encourage— and encourage and encourage—my student leaders to buy a notebook and keep track of how people respond to question 6. That way, at the next meeting, leaders and their groups can talk about how things went that week. I believe it's practicing their faith that counts."

The **Group Talk** questions at the end raise some additional important "real-life" issues and problems that are related to the theme. They offer a good format for group members to give each other practical help and advice.

GETTING STARTED

You may want to use the two introductory sessions to get your group started. The first meeting offers an icebreaker activity and provides an opportunity for participants to get to know each other. The second introductory session uses Acts 2 as an example of how small groups—including yours—should function. These two meetings are extra—they don't count as part of the 31 Bible studies in this book!

Please feel free to contact us at CRC Publications with your comments or questions about *31 More Great Bible Studies for Youth*. You may call us at 1-800-333-8300 or e-mail us at editors@crcpublications.org. If you want to contact the author, we can forward your requests to him. Our hope and prayer is that these materials will be useful to you in your ministry with high school youth.

Author's Comments on Using 31 More Great with Student-Led Groups

These Bible studies are the third in a series that were created for Young Life high school Bible study groups. They can also be used in a number of different settings (see User's Guide for ideas). One goal for these Bible study sheets has been to enable groups of high school students to complete a Bible study without the direct supervision of adult leaders.

As Young Life leaders, we supply donuts for the groups (each person brings three dollars for the year) and then spend time in "big group" singing as well as praises and prayer requests.

After about fifteen or twenty minutes, the groups split up and do the Bible studies. Student leaders know they have wide latitude within their groups. For example, if a member of the group has been through a traumatic experience, the group may need to spend time addressing that need.

I've found that the photocopied handouts usually have much more material than the groups can cover in the thirty-five minutes that are available. So I usually place the studies in the lockers of student leaders one or two days before the meeting. That way they can spend some devotional time with the material and decide what parts of the study they want to use. I firmly tell my leaders never to cut back on reading Scripture in their group meetings and always to spend time praying for each other. Everything else is ancillary.

Students often share leadership of the big group meetings, playing guitars and taking turns leading devotions. It's been my experience that the more you expect students to be involved, the more invested they become.

Each month I have the leaders over for dinner at my house to hang out and to check in. If there are any issues or ideas to discuss, it takes place then. What has become a bit of a mantra in this ministry for me is to remind the student leaders that I am there to serve them and that it is *their* ministry to run for their fellow students.

I use high school seniors as my small group leaders. In choosing leaders, I look at where students are spiritually and how much experience they have in Young Life. I also look to see how involved they are in their churches and how they interact socially. I try very hard never to set someone up to fail. Given the choice between someone who is a charismatic leader and someone who, while not as dynamic, is more spiritually mature, I opt for the latter. I also ask seniors to fill out an evaluation form, which asks why they want to be a leader and what qualifies them.

Ultimately, after choosing one leader per group, I place the other applicants with leaders, asking them to share the leadership with these people. I try to be as inclusive as possible while not damaging the integrity of the group by appointing a leader who will not lead positively.

What has made the groups work—beside the great blessing of God—has been our commitment to giving students permission to lead themselves and to give their own direction to the groups.

We also try to make this a place where young people feel secure. It is not a place where put-downs are allowed (beyond the obvious and familiar type among friends). It's very important that everyone is gladly accepted and made to feel welcome.

While the first two books in this series of *Great* Bible studies were written topically, this third is based on topics suggested by books of the Bible. So in this book, you'll find interesting and relevant information about the writers or about the Bible books themselves sprinkled throughout the studies. Understanding who the audience is for the book of Psalms, for example—God, not us—makes them easier to comprehend.

Also, with the exception of several of the psalms, these lessons have not yet been used in our Young Life Bible studies. I have shown this work to a group of people who are involved in youth ministry (Dave Hodgkinson, Patsy Goers, Crystal Osterink) and to a group of students. To these I say, thanks for all your helpful feedback.

I value your questions and comments (and especially your ideas!). I can be reached at editors@crcpublications.org. The people at CRC Publications will pass your comments along to me, and, if you wish, I can then contact you directly.

Please let me know if I can be of service to you. Thanks.

In Christ's service,
Keith ("Flash") Stulp

Instructions for Student-Led Groups

Welcome to Bible study time! If you're reading this, I'll assume you're part of a group of high school students who are studying the Bible without the supervision of an adult leader.

There are 31 Bible studies from which you can choose (plus two start-up meetings). The studies are clustered around books of the Bible—James, Psalms, Proverbs, Philemon—and the parables of Jesus. It doesn't matter what order you take them in, but once you choose a unit, you'll generally want to take the meetings within that unit in sequence.

Each Bible study is complete on two sides of a single page. Just photocopy and use. No further equipment or knowledge needed. Don't feel that you have to discuss every last question on these sheets. If a question bombs, drop it and move on to the next one. If a question produces some good talk, stay with it for a while.

I suggest you begin with the **Warm-up** questions. There are usually three of these. The first is just an icebreaker to get the group talking to each other. It may or may not have anything to do with the topic. The second and third warm-up questions should take the group into the topic of the meeting.

After the warm-up questions, have group members take turns reading the **introductory comments** in the left-hand column. The comments are meant to introduce the topic and the Bible study on side 2.

On side 2 you'll find a **Scripture passage** and six related **questions.** Before reading Scripture, take a look at question 1—it gives you something to look for while reading. Questions 1-3 help you get at important facts in the passage. Questions 4-6 help you interpret and apply the passage. Question 6 is especially important because it usually asks you to put some part of the Bible study into practice.

The **Group Talk** questions at the end raise some important real-life issues related to the topic. The questions help you exchange ideas, based on your own day-to-day experiences, for solving problems.

That's it. I hope these studies help you grow closer to God and to each other.

In Christ,
Keith ("Flash") Stulp

Start-up Meeting (1)

Hi everyone! Welcome to your small group. Since you're just starting out, it's a good idea to get to know each other better. "The Challenge of Mosts" activity described below is a great way to get started.

THE CHALLENGE OF MOSTS

Pick two of the categories that apply to you best. Take turns sharing your "most whatever" experiences with the group.

most dangerous car ride
most courageous act
most scary moment
most memorable pet story
most amazing athletic feat
most outstanding academic triumph
most unbelievable hunting/fishing adventure
most disastrous dating experience
most disgusting injury
most prestigious award
most (choose your own)

DO THIS, DON'T DO THAT!

In Romans 12:9-18, the apostle Paul gives instructions about how God wants us to live among each other. It's filled with imperatives. Do this, Paul says, but don't do that. Hate what is evil; cling to what's good. Although he was writing to the Roman Christians, he's talking to us too.

For this activity, either divide into pairs (each pair looks at one or two verses), or simply read the passage together verse by verse, stopping after each verse to discuss it. As you read, look at each one of Paul's instructions and think about how it might apply to the way you treat each other within the group. Try to come up with examples for each. For example, "Live in harmony with one another" might mean that you allow other people to express their point of view without putting them down—even if you disagree with them.

Romans 12:9-18

⁹Love must be sincere. Hate what is evil; cling to what is good. ¹⁰Be devoted to one another in brotherly love. Honor one another above yourselves. ¹¹Never be lacking in zeal, but keep your spiritual fervor, serving the Lord. ¹²Be joyful in hope, patient in affliction, faithful in prayer. ¹³Share with God's people who are in need. Practice hospitality.

¹⁴Bless those who persecute you; bless and do not curse. ¹⁵Rejoice with those who rejoice; mourn with those who mourn. ¹⁶Live in harmony with one another. Do not be proud, but be willing to associate with people of low position. Do not be conceited.

¹⁷Do not repay anyone evil for evil. Be careful to do what is right in the eyes of everybody. ¹⁸If it is possible, as far as it depends on you, live at peace with everyone.

Close your meeting by spending a few minutes in prayer for each other.

Start-up Meeting (2)

THE FELLOWSHIP OF BELIEVERS

Hi! Welcome back to the world of small group Bible study. There's no better example of how small groups—including yours—should function than the group described in Acts 2. Today you'll be taking a look at four ways a group of Christians can grow closer to each other and closer to Christ.

Acts 2:42-45

[42]They devoted themselves to the apostles' teaching and to the fellowship, to the breaking of bread and to prayer. [43]Everyone was filled with awe, and many wonders and miraculous signs were done by the apostles. [44]All the believers were together and had everything in common. [45]Selling their possessions and goods, they gave to anyone as he had need.

1. **"They devoted themselves to the apostles' teaching."** What does that mean?

   __ They agreed to study occasionally.
   __ They agreed to study devotedly.
   __ They agreed to study whenever they didn't have anything better to do.

   Talk about some ways your group can help each other be "devoted to the apostles' teaching." List some that can happen in and out of the group setting.

2. **"They devoted themselves . . . to the fellowship."**
   On the continuums below, make a mark at what level you think this group should function:

   smile when you greet each other   ———————————— ignore each other

   spend time together outside group   ———————————— avoid each other

   affirm and encourage each other   ———————————— insult or make fun of each other

   send each other notes and gifts   ———————————— don't put any effort into the group

   Talk about what it means to affirm each other in this Bible study group. Think of one or two rules that need to be in place for the group to function like the group in Acts 2.

3. **"They devoted themselves to . . . the breaking of bread."** For your group, this means

   __ snacking together
   __ sharing each other's food
   __ making sure no one is left out
   __ eating together inside and outside the meeting time
   __ other

   Talk about eating with your group. Will you have snacks during your meetings? Who will bring them? Will you meet together occasionally for meals?

4. **"They devoted themselves . . . to prayer."** What do you think this means for your group?

   __ praying within the group
   __ taking turns praying for each other
   __ praying for each other outside of the group

   Discuss the importance of prayer and keeping each other in prayer. Then close your meeting by praying for the group as you begin this new Bible study.

1 JAMES: PUTTING OUR FAITH INTO ACTION

START HERE →

Being a Sibling Servant

Ever experienced the joy of being compared to someone else? Especially an older brother or sister? Now, occasionally, this can be a joy. I mean, if your older sibling dragged your parents through the wringer, you could be absolutely mediocre and they'd still look at you with broad smiles and a sense of relief. Words like "You got a 'C+'? Well, well! Let's celebrate!" would come rolling out of their mouths.

However, some of us may not have been so fortunate. Let's imagine that you've been blessed with an older sibling who always did everything right. Great grades, great athletic career, popular—she had it all. And then there's you. Even if they don't come right out and say it, you can sense the comparisons— teachers, your parents' friends, and even dear old Mom and Dad. Doesn't always feel good. Now imagine what it would be like if your older brother was "Mr. Perfect"—Jesus himself!

Jesus must have been a tough act to follow. Of course, James also saw Jesus in a different way than most people did. Jesus *was* his older brother. And this must have bugged him on occasion. After all, living with a person makes him or her fairly human to you. Your clothes get washed together, you use the same bathroom. Pretty humanizing stuff.

To be honest, at first James didn't believe in his brother (John 7:5). But after all was said and done, James firmly believed that his brother was who he said he was: the Savior of the world. Notice that James did not start his letter, "James, the half-brother of Jesus." Nope. To him, it was more important that he call himself a "servant" of Jesus. When you think about it, the fact that someone who grew up with him would conclude that he is God in the flesh is pretty compelling evidence that Jesus is who he said is.

During these eight meetings, we'll be looking at what James has to say about living the Christian life—putting what we believe into practice every day in what we say and do. Paying attention to James makes sense. After all, he had the best role model anyone could ever have.

1. Recall an incident when someone in your family did something monumentally goofy (or monumentally great—we don't want to disqualify anything).

2. What does it feel like to be compared to someone else?
   ___ It's a relief.
   ___ It's hard to deal with.
   ___ It's an honor.
   ___ Other: _____

   What do you say when teachers or other adults compare you to someone else?

3. Try to imagine what James would have to say to others about his brother.
   ___ He's not perfect!
   ___ I'm as good as he is!
   ___ Oh yeah? He can't do that.
   ___ Other: _____

warm**UP**

James 1:1

James, a servant of God and of the Lord Jesus Christ,
To the twelve tribes scattered among the nations:
Greetings.

1. As you read this, imagine what kind of person James was. Think of words to describe him.

2. Who might be "the twelve tribes scattered among the nations"? Why call them "scattered"? Are we part of the twelve tribes?

3. What kind of qualities do you associate with the word "servant"?

4. Why do you suppose James used the word "servant" in the opening of his letter as opposed to "brother"?

5. What conclusion do you suppose James came to about Jesus when he called himself "servant"? About himself?

6. What does James's description of himself as a servant suggest to us? Are we servants to anyone? Think about your relationship to your own brothers and sisters in that light. Share one way you'll commit to serving someone in your family this week.

Group Talk

1. Why do we often treat people we know—our brothers and sisters and our parents, for instance—worse than we treat strangers?
2. For James, being Jesus' servant was more important than being his brother. How can we be servants of Jesus in this small group? To other students?

START HERE →

Trials Ain't All Bad
(a.k.a. Less Pity, More Party)

Remember that children's book *Alexander and the Terrible, Horrible, No Good, Very Bad Day?* Seems like everything that could go wrong for our boy Alexander *did* go wrong.

Although the book is kind of funny, it's not so funny when you're having your own very bad day. And usually those kinds of days come in stretches—not just one day. Problems exist. Your favorite grandparent dies. Or you lose a friend in a car wreck. Or your girlfriend breaks up with you and starts dating your best friend. Or your Dad is getting on your case for every little thing. Or your friends seem to be drifting away from you. Or you're way too heavy to look anything like the waifs in the magazines, and you just can't seem to lose any weight. Or you're really skinny, and you feel like the classic ninety-pound weakling ridiculed by girls and guys alike. If only I could be someone else, you think. Then life would be better—much better.

Well, you're not alone. Most of us have thoughts like these some time or another. But like a good coach rallying his team, James doesn't let us wallow in self-pity. He tells us to "count it pure joy" to face suffering—just the opposite of what we'd expect.

Now, don't get the wrong idea. James wasn't a masochist. He didn't *like* pain. Instead, James was a rare individual who judged everything by how it affected his relationship with Jesus. And if suffering helped drive him even closer to Jesus, well, then he could look at that aspect of suffering with joy.

1. Recall a terrible, horrible, no good, very bad day. What were some of the problems?
   ___ no time for breakfast
   ___ car wouldn't start
   ___ late for school
   ___ computer crashed on homework
   ___ best friend's dog bit you
   ___ other: _____

2. What does the expression "Every cloud has a silver lining" mean? Do you buy this philosophy?

3. Think about Jesus' life. Was it characterized more by joy and freedom or by pain and frustration?

James 1:2-8

²Consider it pure joy, my brothers, whenever you face trials of many kinds, ³because you know that the testing of your faith develops perseverance. ⁴Perseverance must finish its work so that you may be mature and complete, not lacking anything. ⁵If any of you lacks wisdom, he should ask God, who gives generously to all without finding fault, and it will be given to him. ⁶But when he asks, he must believe and not doubt, because he who doubts is like a wave of the sea, blown and tossed by the wind. ⁷That man should not think he will receive anything from the Lord; ⁸he is a double-minded man, unstable in all he does.

1. As you read this, think about what "the world"—that is, those who don't follow the way of Jesus—might say. (For example, in verse 5: "If any of you lacks wisdom . . ." the world might say, "he should go to college.")

2. According to James, what do trials teach us? Should we try to get out of them as soon as we can?

3. What do we need to ask God for to get through these times? Why do you suppose that is important?

4. James tells us that we need to accept trials. Suppose we don't agree with James. What other options do we have?

5. What do you have to work hard at? Is it worth it?

6. Share with the group one "trial" you're going through right now. Do you find James's advice comforting or disturbing when you think about your problem?

group Talk

1. Discuss how we can change our attitudes about accepting trials. In light of this passage, is it OK to be hurt or angry by trials?

2. In Psalm 22:1, the psalmist cries out, "My God, my God, why have you forsaken me?" Jesus said the same thing just before he died on the cross. Both showed anguish over God's seeming lack of involvement in their lives. Compare this reaction with what James says. How do you reconcile the two seemingly different reactions?

JAMES: PUTTING OUR FAITH INTO ACTION

START HERE →

warmUP

Playing Favorites

Maybe you've heard of a little book called *All I Really Need to Know I Learned in Kindergarten* by Robert Fulghum. It talks about things like sharing everything and not hitting people and playing fair. Most people who read the book probably say to themselves, "Isn't that nice! That's the way the world is supposed to be." But if you really think about it, you'll have to conclude that for many of us, reality isn't nearly that nice.

The truth is, we aren't always treated very well ourselves. And too often we are at fault. We judge people by what we can gain by knowing them. We cruise by the solitary loser in the cafeteria in order to squeeze another chair around a table already crowded with the wildly popular. We fail to stand up for the kid who's the butt of mean jokes for fear of what others will think.

Our choice of the folks we associate with is important socially, the world tells us. And sometimes we end up treating people in the light of what they can do for us. Not right, says Jesus. "Do unto others as you would have them do unto you." He could have added, "regardless of what you get out of the deal." In this lesson James zeroes in on how we should treat one another.

1. In the book *Anne of Green Gables*, Anne asks Matthew Cuthbert, "Which would you rather be, divinely beautiful, dazzlingly clever, or angelically good?" Which would *you* rather be?

2. Think of a time when you were intentionally (or unintentionally) left out of something. When that happened, what went through your mind?

3. Here is a list of the occupations of some of the people Jesus hung out with. Attach the moniker upper class (UC), middle class (MC), or lower class (LC) to each of them.
   ___religious person
   ___fisherman
   ___tax collector
   ___leper
   ___prostitute
   ___bleeding woman
   ___dead person

James 2:1-9 (The Message)

My dear friends, don't let public opinion influence how you live out your glorious, Christ-originated faith. If a man enters your church wearing an expensive suit, and a street person wearing rags comes in right after him, and you say to the man in the suit, "Sit here, sir; this is the best seat in the house!" and either ignore the street person or say, "Better sit here in the back row," haven't you segregated God's children and proved that you are judges who can't be trusted?

Listen, dear friends. Isn't it clear by now that God operates quite differently? He chose the world's down-and-out as the kingdom's first citizens, with full rights and privileges. This kingdom is promised to anyone who loves God. And here you are abusing these same citizens! Isn't it the high and mighty who exploit you, who use the courts to rob you blind? Aren't they the ones who scorn the new name—"Christian"—used in your baptisms?

You do well when you complete the Royal Rule of the Scriptures: "Love others as you love yourself." But if you play up to these so-called important people, you go against the Rule and stand convicted by it.

1. As you read this, notice who seem to be the bad people and who seem to be the good people.

2. What prompts us to show favoritism to some people over against others?

3. What has God chosen to give those who are down-and-out—the poor—since he doesn't give them money?

4. Maybe we don't make street people sit in the back row at church. But we're not off the hook. Discuss how you and others in your group show discrimination.

5. Think about this statement: Showing favoritism is primarily selfish; it is motivated by what we can get out of the relationship. Do you agree or disagree? Why?

6. How will you make a conscious effort to be less judgmental in the week ahead—at home, at school, in this group?

Group Talk

1. If you treat some people better than others, you are treating some people worse than others. How does this hurt your Christian witness? How can you take pains to avoid showing favoritism?
2. What assumptions do you make when you come across people who are obviously not a part of your usual scene—either very poor or very rich or completely indifferent to fashion or whatever? Does their appearance make a difference in what you think of them?

4 JAMES: PUTTING OUR FAITH INTO ACTION

Faith Goes Hand in Hand with Deeds

Suppose a person you really like or admire from afar comes up to you and says, "Hey, you busy Friday night? Let's hang out together." Then you hear from your friends that he's trash-talking you around school. He ignores you when he sees you, or, worse, makes a point of being rude to you.

Now imagine that an acquaintance calls you her worst enemy. But then she proceeds to lavish you with praise and presents. And whenever you walk into a room, she seems delighted to see you.

Which situation would you rather have to deal with? Exactly. Deeds are much more important than empty words.

That's basically what James is saying about our faith too. We can say we believe in Jesus Christ all we want, but if our daily lives don't give evidence that we follow his teaching, what good is it? But wait a minute, you may be thinking. Doesn't the apostle Paul tell us that our faith is a free gift from God? That we're saved by faith, not deeds? You're right—Paul says we are "justified by faith apart from observing the law" (Rom. 3:28). James isn't disputing this. He's simply saying that once you have faith, it's going to show up in your actions.

It's been said that we have one tongue in our mouths and two tongues in our shoes. And what the tongues in our shoes do says more about who we are than what the tongue in our mouth says.

1. What happened to the guy who kept crying "Wolf!" in that one fairy tale?

2. When people say, "Hey! We should get together sometime!" or, "We should go out for coffee," do you assume that they mean it, or are they just being polite?

3. Do good intentions count if they aren't accompanied by action? Think of an example of an injustice you see in the world and the kind of action it might require of you.

James 2:14-26

1. As you read this, point out the arguments James offers to show that actions are important.

2. What do the demons believe that we believe? What is the difference between their believing and ours?

3. James mentions two people who had great faith. Who were they and how did their actions show their faith?

[14]What good is it, my brothers, if a man claims to have faith but has no deeds? Can such faith save him? [15]Suppose a brother or sister is without clothes and daily food. [16]If one of you says to him, "Go, I wish you well; keep warm and well fed," but does nothing about his physical needs, what good is it? [17]In the same way, faith by itself, if it is not accompanied by action, is dead. [18]But someone will say, "You have faith; I have deeds."

Show me your faith without deeds, and I will show you my faith by what I do. [19]You believe that there is one God. Good! Even the demons believe that —and shudder.

[20]You foolish man, do you want evidence that faith without deeds is useless? [21]Was not our ancestor Abraham considered righteous for what he did when he offered his son Isaac on the altar? [22]You see that his faith and his actions were working together, and his faith was made complete by what he did. [23]And the scripture was fulfilled that says, "Abraham believed God, and it was credited to him as righteousness," and he was called God's friend. [24]You see that a person is justified by what he does and not by faith alone.

[25]In the same way, was not even Rahab the prostitute considered righteous for what she did when she gave lodging to the spies and sent them off in a different direction? [26]As the body without the spirit is dead, so faith without deeds is dead.

4. James says that we don't have faith if it doesn't show up in our deeds. Do you agree or disagree with this statement? Explain why.

5. Think of someone you know who has great faith. How can you tell? What kind of deeds go along with this person's faith?

6. What do your deeds say about your faith? Ask God to give you opportunities to put your faith into practice this week.

Group Talk

1. What obstacles prevent you from letting your faith guide your actions?
2. What effect do your deeds—both good and bad—have on your friends and neighbors in the world who know you are a Christian? What will they think of your faith if your walk doesn't match your talk?
3. Think of a difficult decision you are faced with (or have been faced with). Does your faith make a difference in what you decide to do?

JAMES: PUTTING OUR FAITH INTO ACTION

START HERE ➔ *warm* **UP**

You Can Tame a Tiger, But You Can't Tame a Tongue

Although it happened many years ago, the memory is still all too clear in Antonia's mind. She was in junior high. Her best friend was going through a really hard time at home—her parents were fighting all the time, and her dad was about to lose his job because he had a hard time controlling his temper at work too. She'd confided in Antonia. A few days later, this friend had walked in on a little circle of people clustered around Antonia. Everyone stopped talking at once and stared at her. Antonia flushed with shame. She'd never forget the look of betrayal on her best friend's face.

Maybe you can relate. Some time or another, we've all put our foot in our mouth. We know how it feels to betray a confidence or trash a reputation or curse with the same tongue we use to praise God. Words are incredibly powerful tools that can encourage and affirm but so often discourage, insult, and degrade.

I wonder if God gave us the gift of time, in part, so that the mistakes we've made in the past can slowly disappear from our (and other people's) memory. Even if we don't completely forget, each new second is a fresh start; each new day a new opportunity to live as God wants us to live.

But time goes on and we still make loads of mistakes. Pretty frustrating, isn't it? James touches on all of this in the beginning of chapter 3. What act constantly reminds us of how far we are from being perfect? It's our speaking—the words that come out of our mouths. If you could find someone whose speech was perfectly true, says James, you'd have a perfect person in perfect control.

So what can we do? Try being silent! Think before you speak, and if what you are about to say is not uplifting, don't say it. Your mother was right.

1. Here's a tongue twister: "Twin-screw steel cruiser." How many times can you say it?

2. When we were kids, we used to say, "Sticks and stones may break my bones but words will never hurt me." Is that true? Think back and remember the worst thing someone ever said to you. How did it make you feel?

3. Why is it so hard to control what we say?

James 3:1-12

1. As you read this, look for the things to which James compares the tongue.

2. Why does James warn us not to be in a rush to become teachers?

3. James calls the tongue "a restless evil, full of deadly poison." Why does he single out this small body part for such strong condemnation?

[1]Not many of you should presume to be teachers, my brothers, because you know that we who teach will be judged more strictly. [2]We all stumble in many ways. If anyone is never at fault in what he says, he is a perfect man, able to keep his whole body in check.

[3]When we put bits into the mouths of horses to make them obey us, we can turn the whole animal. [4]Or take ships as an example. Although they are so large and are driven by strong winds, they are steered by a very small rudder wherever the pilot wants to go. [5]Likewise the tongue is a small part of the body, but it makes great boasts. Consider what a great forest is set on fire by a small spark. [6]The tongue also is a fire, a world of evil among the parts of the body. It corrupts the whole person, sets the whole course of his life on fire, and is itself set on fire by hell.

[7]All kinds of animals, birds, reptiles and creatures of the sea are being tamed and have been tamed by man, [8]but no man can tame the tongue. It is a restless evil, full of deadly poison.

[9]With the tongue we praise our Lord and Father, and with it we curse men, who have been made in God's likeness. [10]Out of the same mouth come praise and cursing. My brothers, this should not be. [11]Can both fresh water and salt water flow from the same spring? [12]My brothers, can a fig tree bear olives, or a grapevine bear figs? Neither can a salt spring produce fresh water.

4. Is it possible for us to use our tongues only for blessing others?

5. What do the words we speak indicate about our hearts?

6. What steps will you take this week to try to control the words that come out of your mouth?

Group Talk

1. We've all said things we wish we could un-say—things for which an apology is necessary. Think of someone you need to apologize to. Discuss with the group what you should include in a note of apology. Then write the note, and mail it.
2. Try going for a period of time without saying anything (short of being rude, of course). Next week, describe to the group what it was like.

6 JAMES: PUTTING OUR FAITH INTO ACTION

warm UP

1. Name your favorite action movie. What do you like best about it?

2. What are some of the things that you want but don't get? Why not?

3. Think about the last time you were really angry about something. Was it because you didn't get your own way, or because of some injustice that you noticed? What's the difference?

Choosing Sides

You know the drill. Your sister borrows your favorite sweater without asking (again). You spend five minutes searching for it in your closet, and then you check her room. It's scrunched on the floor underneath a pile of smelly clothes. You track her down and let her have it: "You ALWAYS take my stuff! You're such a slob!..." and on and on and on. By the time you finish yelling at each other, you're both really steamed. About a sweater? By now, that seems beside the point. But all that anger really pumps you up.

Why do we find it so easy to fight with those who are closest to us? Why do we like to win arguments and talk down to people we dislike? Basically, it's the bad part of our human nature crying out to be superior all the time.

James, however, isn't too pleased to see this attitude in Christians. "You're cheating on God," he says. "If all you want is your own way, flirting with the world every chance you get, you end up enemies with God" (*The Message*). What does James see as the cause of this attitude? For one thing, a poor relationship with God that shows itself in a meaningless prayer life. For another, way too much interest in what the world finds important rather than what God finds important.

So what remedy does James suggest? "Yell a loud *no* to the Devil and watch him scamper" (*The Message*). Consider what God has done for us and let God work his will in us. In that frame of mind, it isn't too hard to think of going to God to apologize and mend our ways. And the more we try to pursue God, the easier it gets, says James. These are good words of hope.

It's simple, really. You've got to choose. Do you love the world and its pleasures or do you love God?

James 4:1-10

1. As you read this passage, look for the problem as James defines it and what our response needs to be.

2. What causes fights and quarrels among us? What about wars?

3. Why is it important to resist doing wrong (the devil)?

4. Verse 5 could be translated like this: "The Holy Spirit desires us for himself alone." With whom is the Spirit sharing us?

[1]What causes fights and quarrels among you? Don't they come from your desires that battle within you? [2]You want something but don't get it. You kill and covet, but you cannot have what you want. You quarrel and fight. You do not have, because you do not ask God. [3]When you ask, you do not receive, because you ask with wrong motives, that you may spend what you get on your pleasures.

[4]You adulterous people, don't you know that friendship with the world is hatred toward God? Anyone who chooses to be a friend of the world becomes an enemy of God. [5]Or do you think Scripture says without reason that the spirit he caused to live in us envies intensely? [6]But he gives us more grace. That is why Scripture says:

"God opposes the proud but gives grace to the humble."

[7]Submit yourselves, then, to God. Resist the devil, and he will flee from you. [8]Come near to God and he will come near to you. Wash your hands, you sinners, and purify your hearts, you double-minded. [9]Grieve, mourn and wail. Change your laughter to mourning and your joy to gloom. [10]Humble yourselves before the Lord, and he will lift you up.

5. James tells us that when we turn from our former ways, we'll want to "grieve, mourn and wail." But what if we don't feel bad about living wrong? How can we learn to grieve when we are disappointing God (v. 9)?

6. Think about your relationship to "the world" as evidenced by the way you choose to spend your time, the books you read, the movies you watch. What does it say about your relationship to God? What do you need to work on from today's lesson?

Group Talk

1. Rate your prayer life from 1 (excellent) to 5 (needs work). Discuss how to maintain an active prayer life or how to draw nearer to God if your prayer life needs to be improved.

2. Why does James ask us to change our laughter to mourning and our joy to gloom? Does choosing to submit ourselves to God's will mean walking around with long faces and not having any fun?

7 JAMES: PUTTING OUR FAITH INTO ACTION

START HERE →

warmUP

Including God

Have you ever had this conversation with yourself (or someone else)? "Hmmmm, maybe I'll be a teacher, or maybe I'll go into business." Or perhaps this conversation: "I think I'll try out for the school play and then maybe I'll also get a part-time job." Or even this one: "School gets out early tomorrow. I think I'll go to the mall." These are some pretty normal conversations we have about planning our lives. But notice that they all lack one component. They don't include God.

James got fairly upset with the Christian business folk of his day when they talked of doing this or that and didn't bother asking themselves what God would have them do. It wasn't that James was against making money or moving around, he just was way upset about people thinking they had so much control of their lives that they could do whatever they wanted, and God would bless them no matter what.

The problem with such grandiose thinking is that we begin to believe we're really in charge. Wrong, says James. You think you're such hot stuff. Don't you realize that you're really nothing but a bit of fog, here today and gone tomorrow?

Much better if we pray about our decisions and mean it when we say, "If it is God's will, I'll do this or that." We should not only keep God in our plans, we should seek out God's will about what we should do. And pursuing God's will rather than our own brings not only security, but adventure too. Because with God in charge, we'll be able to do things we couldn't even dream of on our own.

1. Everybody makes plans. What kinds of things do you plan for?
   ___ what I'm going to have for lunch
   ___ who I'm going to ask to the senior prom next year
   ___ what I'm going to major in
   ___ how to explain why I'm going to be home an hour past my curfew
   ___ how many kids I'm going to have
   ___ what I'm doing during Spring Break
   ___ other: _____

2. Think of a decision you've recently had to make. It could be something major, like choosing which parent to live with after a divorce. Or it could be something more ordinary, like choosing to join your friends for a late movie even though you know you'll be home way too late. How did you decide what to do?

3. How does God speak wisdom to us?

James 4:13-17

13Now listen, you who say, "Today or tomorrow we will go to this or that city, spend a year there, carry on business and make money." 14Why, you do not even know what will happen tomorrow. What is your life? You are a mist that appears for a little while and then vanishes. 15Instead, you ought to say, "If it is the Lord's will, we will live and do this or that." 16As it is, you boast and brag. All such boasting is evil. 17Anyone, then, who knows the good he ought to do and doesn't do it, sins.

1. As you read this passage, guess what kind of mood James was in as he wrote. What clues do you have for deciding?

2. What kind of activities were the business folk planning? Is there anything wrong with these?

3. "As it is, you boast and brag." What is James saying these people are boasting and bragging about?

4. What does James imply when he says our lives are a mist? Does that make you feel comforted or helpless? Why?

5. Is God really interested in all of our plans? What parts of our lives don't you think we need to include God in? Give some examples.

6. How do you tell what God wants you to do with your life? How will you figure out God's will for a decision you need to make this week?

Group Talk

1. The Bible tells us to pray continually (1 Thess. 5:17) And Psalm 1 called the person who meditates on the law of the Lord day and night "blessed." Is there a relationship between doing these two things and clueing God in on everything we do?

2. If God cares about everyday things like what movies you watch or how you dress or whom you date, how do you decide what choices to make? Can you be sure you're making the right decisions?

8 JAMES: PUTTING OUR FAITH INTO ACTION

Practicing Patience

What's your basic attitude in life? You can probably sign up for the Myers-Briggs or some other personality test in the guidance office at school to help you learn more about yourself. But even if you've never taken any of these tests, you should be able to figure it out. For instance, are you the laid-back type who takes life as it comes, always content to go along with your friends' plans? Or are you the volcanic type who goes tromping through life at breakneck speed, getting restless easily, and always looking ahead to what's coming next?

Whatever your personality, you'll inevitably bump up against situations that don't work out quite the way you want them to. Maybe you are waiting for something good to happen, and it doesn't. Or maybe something bad happened to you, and it's taking far longer than you think it should to get over it.

At times like that, says James, practice patience. Be like the farmers who patiently wait for the sun and rain to do their work before the harvest comes. Easy for them, you may be grumbling. I'm just not the patient type. But keep this in mind: one of the many great benefits of living in God's kingdom is that we get to let God worry about stuff that is out of our control. God's agenda may not always fit ours, but he does have one. Our job, then, is to learn the art of patience.

Does practicing patience mean doing nothing? No. Not in God's eyes. After all, God's kingdom is not a finished product on this earth. Christians are called to be salt and light in the world—that means standing up for what's right and serving others wherever we are. So take a deep breath, practice patience on what you can't control, and get to work on the rest.

1. What kind of attitude do you identify with most?
___ Frankenstein's Monster
___ Wicked Witch of the West
___ Wile E. Coyote
___ Pollyana
___ other: _____

2. What did you wait a long time to get? Was it worth the wait?
___ a room of your own
___ driver's license
___ an "A" in math
___ a trip to Disney World
___ other: _____

3. Which of these Bible characters had patience? Did it pay off?
___ Joshua
___ Job
___ Thomas

James 5:7-12

1. As you read this, find out why James calls those who practice patience "blessed."

2. When will everything ultimately be set right?

3. What are farmers doing while they are waiting for their crops?

⁷Be patient, then, brothers, until the Lord's coming. See how the farmer waits for the land to yield its valuable crop and how patient he is for the autumn and spring rains. ⁸You too, be patient and stand firm, because the Lord's coming is near. ⁹Don't grumble against each other, brothers, or you will be judged. The Judge is standing at the door!

¹⁰Brothers, as an example of patience in the face of suffering, take the prophets who spoke in the name of the Lord. ¹¹As you know, we consider blessed those who have persevered. You have heard of Job's perseverance and have seen what the Lord finally brought about. The Lord is full of compassion and mercy.

¹²Above all, my brothers, do not swear—not by heaven or by earth or by anything else. Let your "Yes" be yes, and your "No," no, or you will be condemned.

4. How have you experienced God's "compassion and mercy" while practicing patience?

5. James reminds his readers of the prophets who put up with all kinds of hardship while all the time honoring God. What is the reward for people who persevere in patience?

6. Decide on an area in your life where you need to practice. Ask God to help you stand firm.

Group Talk

1. James tells us that we shouldn't complain about each other, or else we will be judged. What does this suggest about how we should treat our friends and family?
2. How do we avoid condemnation? How can our choice of language show that we trust God to care for our lives, down to the last detail?
3. One of your friends has been waiting patiently for years for his brother to be healed of cancer. He and his family and the whole community have been praying faithfully for healing. Now he's getting frustrated. He wonders if God really cares. What do you say to encourage your friend?

1

PSALMS: EXPRESSING OUR EMOTIONS

For or Against?

Ever read someone else's diary? Well, you shouldn't—even if your sister leaves hers lying around in plain view! But if the diary is published as a book, I guess it's OK. Anne Frank's *Diary of a Young Girl,* for instance, is the record of a young Jewish girl's honest, straight-from-the-heart thoughts and feelings, written while she and her family were in hiding from the Nazis during the second World War.

If you haven't read Anne Frank's diary, there's another famous diary you probably have read. It's called the book of Psalms. According to writer Philip Yancey, psalms are "personal prayers in the form of poetry, written by a variety of different people—peasants, kings, professional musicians, rank amateurs—in wildly fluctuating moods" (*The Bible Jesus Read*).

Now, if you've ever written personal stuff in a diary or journal, you know your moods fluctuate all over the place. One day you're way up; the next you are down low. That's the way it is with the psalms, our topic for the next few weeks. Sometimes the psalmists almost go crazy praising God for everything in sight; other times they grumble and grouse about why the good guys suffer while the bad guys live on easy street. And lots of times both things happen in a single psalm. 'Tis a puzzle.

But remember, the psalmists were people like us. They didn't set out to write a catechism book. They just wrote about life and about how they felt about stuff that was happening to them every day. They let God know exactly what they were thinking and how they were feeling. They poured out their praise and their questions and their anger toward God. Why? Because they wanted to talk to God, and because they knew God really wants to hear.

So let's get started with the very first psalm. It's about making a choice, the most important choice of our lives. We have two—and only two—roads to choose from: with God or against God. The psalmist makes it pretty obvious which choice makes the most sense to him.

1. Did you ever read someone else's diary? What caused you to do such a dastardly deed?

2. Think of a parent or one of your best friends. Check all the emotions you have felt regarding this person in the last month.
   ___anger
   ___joy
   ___frustration
   ___sorrow
   ___love
   ___pain
   ___bewilderment
   ___other: _____

3. Although you may have felt all these different emotions, how would you describe the relationship overall?

Psalm 1
(The Message)

How well God must like you—
    you don't hang out at Sin Saloon,
    you don't slink along Dead-End Road,
    you don't go to Smart-Mouth College.

Instead you thrill to GOD's Word,
    you chew on Scripture day and night.
You're a tree replanted in Eden,
    bearing fresh fruit every month,
Never dropping a leaf,
    always in blossom.

You're not at all like the wicked,
    who are mere windblown dust—
Without defense in court,
    unfit company for innocent people.

GOD charts the road you take.
    The road *they* take is Skid Row.

1. As you read this, look for how the writer describes good people and how he describes the wicked.

2. How does the image of a tree "replanted in Eden" help us understand what it's like to be a person who loves God?

3. The psalmist is talking about someone who "thrills to God's Word." What is this person doing?

4. The psalmist seems to be saying that everything you do either moves you closer toward or further from God. (Or closer to or further from trouble.) Do you agree? What difference does this make to the way you make everyday choices?

5. How does verse 6, "GOD charts the road you take," comfort you? Talk about a time when you experienced God watching over you.

6. What will you take from this psalm that will help you during the week ahead?

Group Talk

1. This psalm does not always seem true—it doesn't always match our experience. What mood do you have to be in to appreciate this psalm?
2. Do you "thrill to God's Word"? What kinds of things can you do to share the psalmist's delight in finding out more about God? How does being in this Bible study help you to "chew on Scripture day and night"?

2 PSALMS: EXPRESSING OUR EMOTIONS

START HERE →

warmUP

Why Me?

There's a crude bumper sticker around that says, in effect, "Bad stuff happens." That's a fact—it does. Even to good people. Even to you and me. And when it does, we can't help but ask, Why? Why is this happening to me? Doesn't God care anymore? We feel all alone in the world, deserted by even our friends. It's a rotten feeling. Especially when we've done nothing to deserve all this.

Take comfort in this: there are tons of people in the Bible who felt just the same as you. Job, for example. Add Naomi and David and Elijah. And Jonah. Even Jesus, as he hung dying on the cross. The list is long and distinguished. Be proud that you belong in such a group. For all of us who feel this way, David wrote Psalm 22. It's the most quoted psalm in the New Testament.

And remember this: Although David wrote, "My God, my God, why have you forsaken me?" he didn't stop there. The God who formed the world was in charge then, and in David's mind, God's still in charge. We too can look back at our lives and see the pattern of God's faithfulness. If you look back at the pattern of your life, you'll see it too—just like David did. A God who's in charge. A God who hasn't forgotten us. A God who will never forget us.

1. Have you ever been lost? What happened?

2. Do you think you learn more from winning or from losing?

3. How can you see the pattern of God's faithfulness when you look back at the things that have happened to you?

Psalm 22:1-8, 19-24

1My God, my God, why have you forsaken me?
   Why are you so far from saving me,
   so far from the words of my groaning?
2O my God, I cry out by day, but you do not answer,
   by night, and am not silent.
3Yet you are enthroned as the Holy One;
   you are the praise of Israel.
4In you our fathers put their trust;
   they trusted and you delivered them.
5They cried to you and were saved;
   in you they trusted and were not disappointed.
6But I am a worm and not a man,
   scorned by men and despised by the people.
7All who see me mock me;
   they hurl insults, shaking their heads:
8"He trusts in the LORD;
   let the LORD rescue him.
Let him deliver him,
   since he delights in him."

19But you, O LORD, be not far off;
   O my Strength, come quickly to help me.
20Deliver my life from the sword,
   my precious life from the power of the dogs.
21Rescue me from the mouth of the lions;
   save me from the horns of the wild oxen.
22I will declare your name to my brothers;
   in the congregation I will praise you.
23You who fear the LORD, praise him!
   All you descendants of Jacob, honor him!
   Revere him, all you descendants of Israel!
24For he has not despised or disdained
   the suffering of the afflicted one;
he has not hidden his face from him
   but has listened to his cry for help.

1. As you read, think of words that describe David's mood when he wrote this psalm.

2. What two things seem to be bothering David in this psalm?

3. Why does David compare himself to a worm ("Here I am, a nothing—an earthworm, something to step on, to squash," *The Message*)?

4. Does David say that *if* God rescues him from all this calamity he will praise God, or will he do it regardless?

5. Think of a very hard experience you or your family has gone through. Where did you feel God was through it all (and afterward)?

6. How does Psalm 22 help you get through the difficult situations you're facing or will face?

Group Talk

1. Is it wrong to get angry with God, since God doesn't make mistakes?
2. "Why do bad things happen to good people?" is a question folks have been struggling with throughout the history of Christianity. It's a question that prevents some people from being able to believe in a loving God. How would you answer this question for such a person?

START HERE ➝ *warm*UP

A Safe Hiding Place

It's so easy to lose track of the big picture in the busyness of our everyday lives. How often do we race into the day feeling completely frazzled? Some days we don't have time to brush our teeth or rub the sleep out of our eyes, let alone time to pray or to think about God. And how often do we let the nagging problems of the day get to us? The overdue fines that keep piling up, the scheduling conflicts that make it hard to juggle the after-school job with sports practice, the "D" in German. . . . Stuff like that can make us feel like digging a hole and crawling into it.

If you can relate, then Psalm 46 is for you. It's a psalm that says, "OK, sit down, take a deep breath, and get everything back in perspective."

God was around long before we existed. God holds everything together: the earth, the sky, and even our lives. So, if you are having a bad day, imagine a worse one: mountains falling over; the oceans flooding onto the land; planets spinning out of orbit. Any of these catastrophes would make your day worse, don't you think?

But even if those things were to happen, God is still the One in charge. God is bigger than any problem we can imagine. Whenever we feel like we're being sucked under by the force of a relentless current, God gently reminds us to take some time to reflect on who God is. We can always turn to God for protection and comfort. That's a happy thought. Kind of makes our everyday, garden-variety troubles easier to bear.

1. When you were a child, what were you most scared of?
   ___ monsters under your bed
   ___ the dark
   ___ your older brother
   ___ a mean kid at school
   ___ getting lost
   ___ other: _____

2. Where do you go when you want a happy, peaceful place to get away from it all?

3. Where did Jesus like to hang out when he wanted to be alone?

Psalm 46
(The Message)

God is a safe place to hide,
    ready to help when we need him.
We stand fearless at the cliff-edge of doom,
    courageous in seastorm and earthquake,
Before the rush and roar of oceans,
    the tremors that shift mountains.

    Jacob-wrestling God fights for us,
    GOD of angel armies protects us.

River fountains splash joy, cooling God's city,
    this sacred haunt of the Most High.
God lives here, the streets are safe,
    God at your service from crack of dawn.
Godless nations rant and rave, kings and kingdoms threaten,
    but Earth does anything he says.

    Jacob-wrestling God fights for us,
    GOD of angel armies protects us.

Attention, all! See the marvels of GOD!
    He plants flowers and trees all over the earth,
Bans war from pole to pole,
    breaks all the weapons across his knee.
"Step out of the traffic! Take a long,
    loving look at me, your High God,
    above politics, above everything."

    Jacob-wrestling God fights for us,
    GOD of angel armies protects us.

1. As you read this psalm, look for the disasters mentioned by the psalmist.

2. What kind of place is God's city?

3. What are some of the things God does for us?

4. God wants us to "step out of the traffic" (the NIV says "be still"). Why does Satan want us to hurry?

5. If we believe in the God we read about in Psalm 46, what kind of feelings will we experience less often? What kind will we experience more frequently?

6. Commit yourself to paying attention to God's marvelous presence in the world this week. Next time, share what that was like with the group. What did you notice about God?

Group Talk

1. We often seem to want to carry the world's problems (or at least our own) on our shoulders. How can we remember that God is in charge?
2. Does God cause disasters and catastrophes to happen, or does he allow them? How can we explain them in either case, if God is in charge?

I Did It—I'm Sorry

Perhaps you already know the story line: King David's army is off fighting the enemy, and instead of leading them, King David is chillin' on the roof of his palace. From there he spots his beautiful next-door neighbor Bathsheba taking her bath. King David lusts after her. So he sends for her and gets her pregnant. It gets worse. To cover up this act, he schemes to have Bathsheba's husband (who was faithful and devoted to both his king and his wife) killed. This does not exactly stand out as great behavior from someone whom God called "a man after my own heart."

God sends Nathan the prophet to confront David with his sin, and David repents. Psalm 51 is David's psalm of repentance.

The story doesn't quite end there. David and Bathsheba's infant son dies seven days after his birth, and as a result of David's sin, "the sword" comes upon David's family (2 Sam. 12:10). But God doesn't use this scandal to kick David out of his kingship. Why? Because David was truly penitent.

That's what God wants from us too. No excuses, no blaming others, just a full acknowledgment of our sin. When we blow it big-time, we need to admit it. And when we do, God is willing to forgive us and help us move on. Just as he did for David and Bathsheba, who had another son after all this—a son named Solomon.

1. When it comes to repentance, who are your role models?
   ___ Bart Simpson
   ___ your parents
   ___ Dennis Rodman
   ___ Bill Clinton
   ___ Zacchaeus
   ___ other: _____

2. Did your folks ever catch you trying to hide something you were doing that was wrong? What was the fallout?

3. These Bible characters committed some pretty outstanding sins. What was the fallout in each case?
   a. Judas
   b. Peter
   c. Jonah
   d. Eve

Psalm 51:1-6, 10-12, 17

1. As you read this, look for what David asks God to do for him.

2. What kind of person does David think of himself as?

___very good
___kind of good
___kind of bad—
    makes some
    mistakes
___very bad

3. What kind of person asks for mercy?

___rich person
___poor person
___person with
    nothing to offer
___other: _____
    _____

¹Have mercy on me, O God,
        according to your unfailing love;
according to your great compassion
        blot out my transgressions.
²Wash away all my iniquity
        and cleanse me from my sin.
³For I know my transgressions,
        and my sin is always before me.
⁴Against you, you only, have I sinned
        and done what is evil in your sight,
so that you are proved right when you speak
        and justified when you judge.
⁵Surely I was sinful at birth,
        sinful from the time my mother conceived me.
⁶Surely you desire truth in the inner parts;
        you teach me wisdom in the inmost place.

¹⁰Create in me a pure heart, O God,
        and renew a steadfast spirit within me.
¹¹Do not cast me from your presence
        or take your Holy Spirit from me.
¹²Restore to me the joy of your salvation
        and grant me a willing spirit, to sustain me.

¹⁷The sacrifices of God are a broken spirit;
        a broken and contrite heart,
        O God, you will not despise.

4. David knows he has sinned against God, which is very bad. However, who else did David's sin affect? Name six other people or groups.

5. Describe David's attitude before the incident with Bathsheba and afterward. Perhaps we don't always feel as penitent as we should for our own sins. How can we become more penitent?

6. Share how you feel when you do something wrong. How do you find relief from your guilt or any other feelings you have?

Group Talk

1. God desires a heart that is broken. Why do we always want to appear as if we have it all together?
2. Is a guilty conscience a good or bad thing? How can we use guilty consciences to our advantage?
3. Often when we pray, we ask God to forgive our sins in a very general sort of way. This week resolve to come clean for specific wrongdoing, the way David did. Next time you meet, take a few minutes to talk about what this was like. Was it hard? How did it make you feel?

5

PSALMS: EXPRESSING OUR EMOTIONS

START HERE →

*warm*UP

The Big Picture

Ever have trouble praying? Sometimes it's fairly easy to come up with a list of stuff to pray about: good health, Grandma's lumbago, meeting the soul mate of your dreams, passing French.... But there's another part of prayer—the part sometimes called "adoration" (as in, "Our Father who art in heaven, hallowed be thy name")—that can be a lot harder to come up with. If this is true for you, Psalm 91 can get you thinking in the right direction. It's loaded with images of God's protection and care for us.

God is on our side, says the psalmist. If we are doing God's will in our lives, we can be bold. God is watching our backs.

Perhaps this psalm seems like overkill to you. Maybe you're thinking, Come on! Bad stuff happens to good people all the time. My aunt, for instance. She just died of breast cancer—only forty-three, and she's got three little kids. And what about the high school junior who broke his back playing football? Not only was he a great player—he's a cool person. Good student. Volunteers as a Big Brother on weekends.

If that's what you're thinking, you're right. You won't find any Scripture passage that promises Christians an easy life or one that's pain-free. But just try telling that to the psalmist! He's focused on the big picture. He's got no fear. He's simply in awe of what God has done for him. That's a snapshot of God we should carry with us too!

1. Where (and with what and whom) do you like to relax?

2. What's ever happened to you that scared the bejeebies right out of you?

3. Have you ever found yourself in a position (spiritually or otherwise) in which only God could save you?

Psalm 91:1-6, 9-16

1. As you read this psalm, look for the images the psalmist uses to describe what God is like.

2. According to the psalmist, what don't we need to fear anymore?

3. Who else besides God will help us face perils?

¹He who dwells in the shelter of the Most High
    will rest in the shadow of the Almighty.
²I will say of the LORD, "He is my refuge and my fortress,
    my God, in whom I trust."
³Surely he will save you from the fowler's snare
    and from the deadly pestilence.
⁴He will cover you with his feathers,
    and under his wings you will find refuge;
    his faithfulness will be your shield and rampart.
⁵You will not fear the terror of night,
    nor the arrow that flies by day,
⁶nor the pestilence that stalks in the darkness,
    nor the plague that destroys at midday.

⁹If you make the Most High your dwelling—
    even the LORD, who is my refuge—
¹⁰then no harm will befall you,
    no disaster will come near your tent.
¹¹For he will command his angels concerning you
    to guard you in all your ways;
¹²they will lift you up in their hands,
    so that you will not strike your foot against a stone.
¹³You will tread upon the lion and the cobra;
    you will trample the great lion and the serpent.
¹⁴"Because he loves me," says the LORD, "I will rescue him;
    I will protect him, for he acknowledges my name.
¹⁵He will call upon me, and I will answer him;
    I will be with him in trouble,
    I will deliver him and honor him.
¹⁶With long life will I satisfy him
    and show him my salvation."

4. Which image of God do you relate to best?

5. Who does God protect (vv. 9-10)? How can this be true even when it doesn't seem that way?

6. Share an experience when God rescued you from some kind of trouble. Were you afraid? What lesson did you learn from this experience?

Group Talk

1. How does focusing on these images of God bring us closer to him?
2. Psalm 90:7-9 says, "We are consumed by [God's] anger.... We finish our lives with a moan." How can Psalms 90 and 91 both be true at the same time?

6

PSALMS: EXPRESSING OUR EMOTIONS

START HERE ➝

When It's OK to Curse

It's probably a good thing we don't say everything we think. Scratch that. It's a *very* good thing we don't say everything we think ... to the little old lady who's driving twenty in a zone where the speed limit is thirty-five ... or to the guy with four little kids who cuts in front of you at McDonald's. On those occasions, we're better off biting our tongue, hard as it may be.

The psalmists, though, don't always demonstrate that kind of restraint. They rail against evil people with a passion that makes us cringe. Their desire for bad stuff to happen to their enemies sounds pretty mean, to say the least. Consider this, for example: "May his children be beggars; may they be driven from their ruined homes" (Ps. 109:10). Or "Happy is he ... who seizes your infants and dashes them against the rocks" (Ps. 137:8-9).

These wishes sound downright barbaric. At the very least, they strike us as being contrary to what Jesus teaches in the gospels about loving your enemy.

But the truth is, they are a part of the psalms. And they belong there. Remember that we are not the audience for these psalms, God is. Try to put yourself in the psalmists' shoes: if truly evil people have taken your land or killed your children and made slaves of you and your family, God is really the only court in the world where you can go with your grievances. We don't have to look far back in our own history to see atrocities like this: think of the Holocaust. Or the killings in Rwanda. Or the shootings at Columbine.

So the next time you're angry or hurt or confused, don't hide it from God. After all, God's the only one who can do something about your pain. And God's listening.

Warm UP

1. What kind of stuff makes you really steamed?
   ___ surprise quizzes
   ___ friends who "borrow" stuff and never give it back
   ___ being lectured by your mom for something you didn't even do
   ___ drivers who tailgate
   ___ bullies who pick on little kids
   ___ other: _____

2. In what ways can we get back at someone who has wronged us?

3. How do you treat someone who has mistreated you? Is it OK to get mad, or are we supposed to "turn the other cheek" (to use Jesus' expression)?

Psalm 137

1. As you read this, find out who the psalmist is addressing.

2. What do the Babylonians ask the Israelites to do? Why is this both difficult and insulting?

3. What have the Babylonians done to Jerusalem? Why would this be especially hard on a Jewish person?

¹By the rivers of Babylon we sat and wept
    when we remembered Zion.
²There on the poplars
    we hung our harps,
³for there our captors asked us for songs,
    our tormentors demanded songs of joy;
    they said, "Sing us one of the songs of Zion!"

⁴How can we sing the songs of the LORD
    while in a foreign land?
⁵If I forget you, O Jerusalem,
    may my right hand forget its skill.
⁶May my tongue cling to the roof of my mouth
    if I do not remember you,
if I do not consider Jerusalem
    my highest joy.

⁷Remember, O LORD, what the Edomites did
    on the day Jerusalem fell.
"Tear it down," they cried,
    "tear it down to its foundations!"

⁸O Daughter of Babylon, doomed to destruction,
    happy is he who repays you
    for what you have done to us—
⁹he who seizes your infants
    and dashes them against the rocks.

4. What course of action can we take if we have been wronged by another person?

5. Think of something that makes you angry. How do you express your anger and frustration to God?

6. What does this psalm teach you about the character of God? Does knowing this help you in any way?

group Talk

1. How do you explain the psalmist's desire for revenge on his enemies in the light of Jesus' teachings about loving our enemies?
2. Suppose your neighbor tells you he doesn't think much of the Christian God because so much of the Old Testament, including the Psalms, talks about situations that are violent and horrible. What do you say?

7 PSALMS: EXPRESSING OUR EMOTIONS

START HERE →

warmUP

On Our Way

Remember Dorothy in the movie *The Wizard of Oz?* She and her little dog Toto, along with their companions the Lion, the Tin Man, and the Scarecrow, spend much of the movie traveling to the Emerald City to find the wizard—the great and powerful Oz. Along the way they run into all kinds of obstacles (including apple-throwing trees and the Wicked Witch of the West). By following the yellow brick road and relying on their own strength and courage, they eventually make it to their destination.

Psalm 121 is a psalm for those who are on a journey. But it has a different focus than the movie. It's not about setting out on a journey to find the great and powerful God. Instead, it celebrates the fact that God goes with us on our journey! Unlike Dorothy and her companions, we aren't traveling on our own. We don't have to rely on our wits and whatever friends we may make along the way. Because God is right there with us every step of the way. We can rely on God.

This "journey psalm" ends this short series on the psalms. We've looked at psalms of wisdom (1), despair (22), safety (46), forgiveness (51), confidence in God (91), and rage (137). I hope you've discovered that no matter what you're feeling and thinking, there are psalms that speak to you and help you speak to God. I want you to know that God is walking with you wherever you go. He's with you whether the road is smooth or full of potholes. He's with you through every switchback and detour. Wherever you are on your way—in the highest mountains or in the valley of the shadow of death—you can be sure God is there.

1. Describe a lousy thing has happened to you on a trip—be it a family vacation, class trip, or whatever.

2. Did anyone ever save you from a jam? Describe the person who
   ___ opened your car door with a hanger
   ___ saved you from a fight with two big guys
   ___ fixed your car when it broke down on the highway
   ___ gave you $5 in the checkout line when you were short
   ___ other: _____

3. What miraculous things have you personally seen God do?

psalm 121

¹I lift up my eyes to the hills—
        where does my help come from?
²My help comes from the LORD,
        the Maker of heaven and earth.
³He will not let your foot slip—
        he who watches over you will not slumber;
⁴indeed, he who watches over Israel
        will neither slumber nor sleep.
⁵The LORD watches over you—
        the LORD is your shade at your right hand;
⁶the sun will not harm you by day,
        nor the moon by night.
⁷The LORD will keep you from all harm—
        he will watch over your life;
⁸the LORD will watch over your coming and going
        both now and forevermore.

1. As you read this, look for two phrases that are repeated through the psalm. What are they?

2. From what type of stuff does God protect us?

3. What steps does God take to protect us?

4. Since God watches over us all the time, what risks do you think you can take?

___go bungee jumping
___invite a new kid to hang out with you and your friends
___go rock climbing without any safety equipment
___try out for a part in the school play even though you've never acted before
___other: _____

5. Why is worrying bad for us, spiritually or otherwise?

6. Do you believe the psalmist when he says, "The LORD will keep you from all harm"? If that statement is true, why do you or the ones you love still sometimes get hurt?

group Talk

1. When you're dealing with problems, do you ever feel like Dorothy—that is, you've got to figure things out by yourself? Why might this be bad for your spiritual health?
2. What does God do for us that we tend to take for granted? Think of some ways to become more grateful for what God has done for us.
3. Are we responsible for taking care of ourselves? How does that fit with trusting in God to take care of us?

1 PARABLES: JESUS THE STORYTELLER

START HERE →

Jesus' Code Language

Did you and your friends ever make up a secret language? You know, when "difulgunk" meant, "Meet me behind Miss Rauzer's classroom at break," and "bumbloaf" meant, "You owe me your best snack." Or maybe you can remember sending in your Choco-Blast cereal box tops for a free secret decoder ring. The idea of communicating in a private language no one else can understand is mighty appealing.

Jesus didn't use any mumbo-jumbo secret language, though. He was a great storyteller. It wasn't for nothing that crowds followed him around. In fact, sometimes all those people hanging on every word got to be too much for him, and he'd ask his disciples to row him off in a boat. But it's true that few people in his audience seemed to fully understand the stories Jesus was telling.

Jesus often told stories called parables to teach people. They were about everyday situations and folks his audience could relate to—stories about farmers, fishermen, land owners, and Samaritans. You may have heard parables described as "earthly stories with a heavenly meaning," but that's not quite right. The stories Jesus told had an *earthly* meaning. They were meant to teach people about the kingdom of God, which is right here already in this world.

But sometimes Jesus directed his teaching only toward those who truly believed in him. Jesus knew that unless people had faith, his parables about the kingdom of God wouldn't make any sense. In this first parable—the Parable of the Sower—Jesus compares the good news about the kingdom of God to seeds that are scattered on different kinds of ground. He looks at how people respond to that good news.

For the next few sessions, we'll look at some of the parables Jesus told (there were twenty-seven altogether) and what they have to tell us about the kingdom of God.

1. Did you have any special codes for communicating with your friends when you were a kid?

2. Remember trying to grow seeds in little paper cups on the window ledge in kindergarten? How well did the plant turn out?

3. Jesus offers "abundant life" to everyone. How do you suppose he reacts when people reject it? How would you react if you gave someone you love a gift and he or she said, "No thanks"?

Matthew 13:1-13 (The Message)

At about that same time Jesus left the house and sat on the beach. In no time at all a crowd gathered along the shoreline, forcing him to get into a boat. Using the boat as a pulpit, he addressed his congregation, telling stories.

"What do you make of this? A farmer planted seed. As he scattered the seed, some of it fell on the road, and birds ate it. Some fell in the gravel; it sprouted quickly but didn't put down roots, so when the sun came up it withered just as quickly. Some fell in the weeds; as it came up, it was strangled by the weeds. Some fell on good earth, and produced a harvest beyond his wildest dreams.

"Are you listening to this? Really listening?"

The disciples came up and asked, "Why do you tell stories?"

He replied, "You've been given insight into God's kingdom. You know how it works. Not everybody has this gift, this insight; it hasn't been given to them. Whenever someone has a ready heart for this, the insights and understandings flow freely. But if there is no readiness, any trace of receptivity soon disappears. That's why I tell stories: to create readiness, to nudge the people toward receptive insight. In their present state they can stare till doomsday and not see it, listen till they're blue in the face and not get it."

1. As you read this, look for the different kinds of "soil" in which the farmer sows the seed. Describe each type of ground as you come across it.

2. Who is responsible for planting the seed? Who is responsible for making the plants grow?

3. Who is Jesus' audience? Do they understand the parable? Do the disciples understand it?

4. Why are some people given the gift of insight into God's kingdom while others are not? What responsibility do we have toward those who do not have faith?

5. How well does the seed of the gospel flourish in your life? Are you more like the road? The gravel? The weeds? The good earth?

6. Share with the group what it means to you that the kingdom of God is here right now. What difference does it make in the way you choose to live each day?

Group Talk

1. Why do you suppose some people don't want to talk about Jesus? What can we do for these people?
2. What is the basic point of this parable?
3. Describe some evidence of the harvest that comes when the seed of the gospel grows in good soil in your own life and in your community.

2 PARABLES: JESUS THE STORYTELLER

Not Fair!

Maybe you've been working for a year or more slinging burgers at the local Burger Barn or bagging groceries at Foodmart. Or maybe you're just thinking about signing on somewhere one of these days. Either way, you probably have some ideas about what kind of boss you'd like to have. If you're already pulling in a paycheck, you've discovered that a kind and generous boss is better than a mean and stingy one. It's a concept most of us can relate to.

Jesus' disciples were kind of proud of themselves that they left everything to follow Jesus. But they also wanted to know what they'd get out of the deal. Peter, never one to mince words, popped the question. "Tell us, Jesus, what's in it for us?" (Matt. 19:27). In response, Jesus told the story of the boss and the workers in the vineyard.

The bottom line of the parable? At the end of the day, when it's time to pay up, the boss chooses to be generous to everyone. He gives the same amount of money to everybody who worked for him. Those who barely had time to work up a sweat because they started an hour from quitting time got as much as those who slaved all day under a scorching sun. Not surprisingly, that doesn't go over big with the all-day workers.

But think about it. Do any of us deserve God's grace? Have we really "earned" the right to heaven? Isn't it only because God generously chooses to reward us— not according to what we've done but according to his grace—that we receive the ultimate prize, eternal life?

So instead of whining when someone else gets the same reward—someone we think less deserving than ourselves—we can be grateful. God isn't fair. Instead, he's gracious and compassionate.

1. What's the worst thing that has ever happened to you at work (either a paid job or the work you do around the house for your parents)?

2. How do you react if someone who hasn't worked nearly as hard as you have gets as much (or more) praise as you do from your boss?
   ___ upset
   ___ not a big deal
   ___ what happens to the other person doesn't affect me
   ___ other: _____

Matthew 20:1-16

1. As you read this, figure out how many hours each of the workers put in.

2. What were the workers complaining about? Did they have a right to complain?

3. How did the landowner respond?

___angry
___threatening
___understanding
___compassionate
___ other

1"For the kingdom of heaven is like a landowner who went out early in the morning to hire men to work in his vineyard. 2He agreed to pay them a denarius for the day and sent them into his vineyard.

3"About the third hour he want out and saw others standing in the marketplace doing nothing. 4He told them, 'You also go and work in my vineyard, and I will pay you whatever is right.' 5So they went.

"He went out again about the sixth hour and the ninth hour and did the same thing. 6About the eleventh hour he went out and found still others standing around. He asked them, 'Why have you been standing here all day long doing nothing?'

7"'Because no one has hired us,' they answered.

"He said to them, 'You also go and work in my vineyard.'

8"When evening came, the owner of the vineyard said to his foreman, 'Call the workers and pay them their wages, beginning with the last ones hired and going on to the first.'

9"The workers who were hired about the eleventh hour came and each received a denarius. 10So when those came who were hired first, they expected to receive more. But each one of them also received a denarius. 11When they received it, they began to grumble against the landowner. 12'These men who were hired last worked only one hour,' they said, 'and you have made them equal to us who have borne the burden of the work and the heat of the day.'

13"But he answered one of them, 'Friend, I am not being unfair to you. Didn't you agree to work for a denarius? 14Take your pay and go. I want to give the man who was hired last the same as I gave you. 15Don't I have the right to do what I want with my own money? Or are you envious because I am generous?'

16"So the last will be first, and the first will be last."

4. Was the landlord ever untrue to his word? Did he treat the workers fairly?

5. "So the last will be first and the first will be last." What did Jesus mean by this? Who are the "first" and the "last"?

6. What does God's generosity to us teach you about what life is supposed to be like in the kingdom of God? Resolve to carry out what you've learned in the weeks ahead.

Group Talk

1. Why do we always want to be treated better than others (we want the best seat, the best parking spot, the first place in line, the biggest piece of chocolate cake)?

2. Doesn't being a follower of Jesus mean we need to practice the opposite attitude? Discuss as a group how to conquer some of these selfish motives.

3 PARABLES: JESUS THE STORYTELLER

START HERE →

God's Love

Ever take a moment to be amazed at how great God is? Think about it. That you're reading this lesson right now (or listening to someone else read it) is a tribute to the mind God gave you. That you are wearing nice clothes in a nice room with these nice friends shows how God takes care of you. That you can walk outside and see bugs and birds and trees and clouds and sky and weather and everything else are clues that should tell you how much God thinks of you.

Someone said once that God waits impatiently for each of us to be born so he can have a conversation with us. Imagine that—the Creator who spoke this whole lovely world and all the galaxies and every blade of grass into being is waiting to hear from *you*.

One thing, though—God won't wait for you forever. There is a limit to God's patience. God is calling you. And sooner or later you've got to say yes, or it will be too late.

Jesus told this story about the tenants in a vineyard to the religious leaders of the day—the chief priests, the teachers of the law, and the elders. These people saw Jesus as a serious threat to their whole way of life. Ultimately, Jesus knew, they'd kill him. This story was his way of saying, "Listen up, people. God won't allow weeds to grow in his vineyard forever. He's going to do away with those who try to ruin everything."

So listen up! Learn what God expects of you when you're working in his vineyard. You'll be glad you did.

1. Has there ever been a time that you've gotten lost or separated from the people you were with—like on a road trip or at an amusement park? Or maybe even a time that your getting separated wasn't an accident—you were "ditched"? How did it feel?

2. When's the last time you were bowled over by the beauty and power of God's creation? Was it the intense greens of early spring after a bare, brown winter that got to you, or a spectacular butterfly, or a neon sunset at the beach? What do such things tell us about God?

3. No doubt you've heard the expression "When the cat's away, the mice will play." Why do you think it might be harder to do something you're supposed to do when the person in charge leaves you alone?

Mark 12:1-9

1. As you read this, look for ways the tenants rejected the owner.

2. What was the condition of the vineyard as the owner left it when he went on a journey?

___neglected
___dirty
___orderly
___profitable

3. Who do the following people in the parable represent?

a. owner
b. tenants
c. servants
d. owner's son

¹He then began to speak to them in parables: "A man planted a vineyard. He put a wall around it, dug a pit for the winepress and built a watchtower. Then he rented the vineyard to some farmers and went away on a journey. ²At harvest time he sent a servant to the tenants to collect from them some of the fruit of the vineyard. But they seized him, beat him and sent him away empty-handed. ⁴Then he sent another servant to them; they struck this man on the head and treated him shamefully. ⁵He sent still another, and that one they killed. He sent many others; some of them they beat, others they killed.

⁶"He had one left to send, a son, whom he loved. He sent him last of all, saying, 'They will respect my son.'

⁷"But the tenants said to one another, 'This is the heir. Come, let's kill him, and the inheritance will be ours.' ⁸So they took him and killed him, and threw him out of the vineyard.

⁹"What then will the owner of the vineyard do? He will come and kill those tenants and give the vineyard to others."

4. What kinds of "fruit of the vineyard" does God want to collect from us? What happens if we don't have anything to show for ourselves?

5. How long will God be patient with the tenants in the vineyard? With us?

6. What did you learn from this parable? How will it affect the way you do your work at home and school and on the job?

Group Talk

1. What are some of the things you do that get in the way of having a great relationship with God? Ask your group to suggest ways to overcome these obstacles.
2. In what ways do we make Jesus and his servants welcome or unwelcome in our lives?
3. How would you explain what God wants from us to someone who doesn't know God?

Who's My Neighbor?

What do I need to do to get eternal life? That's the question a scholar who majored in religious studies asked Jesus one day. Jesus answered his question with another: What does the Bible say? That's easy, replied the scholar (you can bet he knew his Ten Commandments inside and out). Love the Lord your God and love your neighbor as yourself. Bingo! said Jesus. There's your answer. Do it and you'll live.

Well then, who is my neighbor? the scholar wanted to know. Then Jesus told the parable of the good Samaritan.

The scholarly type was probably hoping for a nice tight definition he could use to plot his way into eternal life. If so, this parable must have blown him away. First, Jesus' story makes it clear that *anyone in need* is our neighbor. Whoa! Think about the number of people in this world who are in need. That would be roughly the same number as there are people—at last count, over six billion. Our neighbors include the know-it-all in math class, the popular girl who wears only the hottest stuff, the millionaire whose name graces half the buildings in town, and the coke addict on the street corner.

Second, it's pretty obvious that there are more needs out there than we could ever hope to meet. It's also obvious that even if we win the Nobel prize for charity, we can never earn our salvation. It's a gift from God, plain and simple. And the best way we can thank God for the gift is to try and live like Christ in this world.

What does that take? It's simple and it's hard. It takes everything we have, every minute of our lives.

1. Have you ever picked up a hitchhiker? Why or why not?

2. You're riding on the city bus when a bag lady gets on and chooses the seat opposite you. She's dressed in rags, and it's all too obvious she hasn't taken a shower for a very long time. All of a sudden, she quits mumbling to herself and starts talking to you. What do you do?

___ stare straight ahead and pretend you don't hear

___ move to another seat

___ invite her to your home for a bath

___ chat with her and get off at the next stop

___ ask her some questions about her life

___ other: _____

3. What do you think eternal life has to do with being neighborly?

Luke 10:30-37
(The Message)

1. As you read this, look for the things the Samaritan does for the wounded man.

2. The Jews hated Samaritans. Why is this important to the story?

3. With whom in the story would the religious expert have identified? What advice does Jesus have for him?

Just then a religion scholar stood up with a question to test Jesus. "Teacher, what do I need to do to get eternal life?"

He answered, "What's written in God's Law? How do you interpret it?"

He said, "That you love the Lord your God with all your passion and prayer and muscle and intelligence—and that you love your neighbor as well as you do yourself."

"Good answer!" said Jesus. "Do it and you'll live."

Looking for a loophole, he asked, "And just how would you define 'neighbor'?"

Jesus answered by telling a story. "There was once a man traveling from Jerusalem to Jericho. On the way he was attacked by robbers. They took his clothes, beat him up, and went off leaving him half-dead. Luckily a priest was on his way down the same road, but when he saw him he angled across to the other side. Then a Levite religious man showed up; he also avoided the injured man.

"A Samaritan traveling the road came on him. When he saw the man's condition, his heart went out to him. He gave him first aid, disinfecting and bandaging his wounds. Then he lifted him on to his donkey, led him to an inn, and made him comfortable. In the morning he took out two silver coins and gave them to the innkeeper, saying, 'Take good care of him. If it costs any more, put it on my bill—I'll pay you on my way back.'

"What do you think? Which of the three became a neighbor to the man attacked by robbers?"

"The one who treated him kindly," the religion scholar responded.

Jesus said, "Go and do the same."

4. When the Samaritan saw the injured man, his "heart went out to him," and he stopped and took care of him. What keeps us from doing the same thing?

5. How do we sometimes try to justify walking past people in need? Are any of these excuses valid?

6. Think of someone you know who needs your help or your attention or your time or your comfort. What can you do to follow the Samaritan's example? Share your ideas with the group.

Group Talk

1. It's easy to do stuff for people we like. Why does Jesus insist that we help people we have reason to hate?

2. Sometimes thinking about the needs people have can be overwhelming. Poverty, for instance, may seem like too big a problem for you to make any difference. How can this be a copout for doing anything at all? Discuss specific ways you can help address a big problem.

START HERE →

warmUP

Whose Is It Anyway?

Somebody in the crowd came up to Jesus with a request. "Hey, Jesus," he said, "make my brother share his inheritance with me. Why should he get to keep it all?" Jesus didn't give the guy much satisfaction. Instead he gave him a lecture about being greedy. And then he told this story about a rich man who had so much stuff he had to tear down his barns and build bigger ones to store his stuff in.

Jesus' warning about greed is one we need to hear over and over again. Because the sad fact about our culture is that "stuff" is key. We are what we own and what we look like. And we judge others by the same standards. Who are the popular kids in your school? Probably the rich kids. And we'd like to be more like them. Most of us would like our clothes to come with names like Abercrombie and Banana Republic, even if the family budget is K-Mart and Goodwill. We'd sooner stay home than be caught driving the family minivan.

Don't get the wrong idea here. Jesus wasn't against wealth. After all, he created us with the ability to make and acquire stuff. It's just that he knew that having a lot of stuff can become a major headache. "Don't forget," says Jesus, "your life isn't defined by what you have." Jesus knew what we sometimes forget: when we focus too much on what we have or what we wish we had, it's hard to put God first. A foolish trade-off, the parable makes clear.

Makes sense. Because when you die, you won't walk into heaven loaded down with all your favorite things. The truth is, you'll leave this world pretty much the way you came in—with just your skin. No stuff. What will count then is how rich you are toward God. That happens when you love others and live for God. And to do that, you don't need a lot of stuff.

1. What kind of stuff do you really wish you could have?
   ___ the latest computer, complete with CD burner
   ___ a certain cool brand of shoes
   ___ a shiny red Volkswagen Bug
   ___ a healthy bank account
   ___ a new guitar
   ___ other: _____

2. Is having more than enough of everything a mark of God's favor?

3. For a while there, *Who Wants to Be a Millionaire?* was the most popular show on TV. What's our fascination with being rich? Does having lots of stuff make us happy?

Luke 12:16-21

1. As you read this, find out who the rich man serves.

2. What is God's response to this man?

3. The rich man thought he had it made. "Hey, now I can take it easy and enjoy life," he said to himself. What's wrong with this attitude?

16And he told them this parable: "The ground of a certain rich man produced a good crop. 17He thought to himself, 'What shall I do? I have no place to store my crops.'

18"Then he said, 'This is what I'll do. I will tear down my barns and build bigger ones, and there I will store all my grain and my goods. 19And I'll say to myself, "You have plenty of good things laid up for many years. Take life easy; eat, drink and be merry."'

20"But God said to him, 'You fool! This very night your life will be demanded from you. Then who will get what you have prepared for yourself?'

21"This is how it will be with anyone who stores up things for himself but is not rich toward God."

4. Verses 18-19 describe what the rich man decides to do. Rewrite those two verses to show what he might have said that would have been pleasing to God.

5. Greed—wanting more and more stuff—is a powerful force we're all familiar with. Why do we keep wanting things? Is it ever possible to have so much stuff that you don't want any more?

6. What's your own attitude toward your possessions? Are you in danger of storing up stuff at the expense of living a godly life? What will you do about it?

group Talk

1. What attitude should we have about our stuff? Can having lots of things make us happy?
2. In our society, there is a huge gap between the rich and the poor. Discuss how you could start using your resources to serve others in concrete ways. Is your group willing to work on some kind of group project—a food drive, a workday to help shut-ins in your neighborhood, a tutoring program?

6 PARABLES: JESUS THE STORYTELLER

warmUP

Meeting Jesus

Ask ten people this question: If Jesus were to step out of a car and walk right up to you, what would he say to you? You might be surprised by some of the answers. Many people imagine that Jesus would say something that would make them feel guilty. "He'd say I should try harder." Or, "He'd tell me to pray more."

Those of us who have been raised to live good, moral lives can probably relate. The problem with living *good* lives is that we can always live *better* lives, and this idea creeps into our deepest selves.

Even though we know that our salvation is a free gift—we can't earn it no matter how many good things we do—we can't help but feel that we aren't doing enough. In spite of ourselves, we begin to equate our faith with being a good person. We begin to believe that people who go to church and youth group regularly, who are always helpful and polite, who are never home past their curfew, who always do their homework on Friday instead of saving it till Sunday night set the standards. And the rest of us never quite measure up.

Fortunately for us, the God of the Bible doesn't see it that way. The God of the Bible (shown to us in the person of Jesus) loves us way too much. Our God doesn't stand around with arms crossed tightly, tapping his foot with an angry scowl as we constantly screw up. If anything, God looks hurt and grieved when we mess up—not so much for himself, but for us. And when we come back to our senses, he's ready to throw a party!

1. What would Jesus say to you if you were all alone right now and he stepped into the room? Take a moment to write down the conversation.

2. How do you feel when you know you've blown it big-time and you're sure your parents are going to ground you for a month, but they end up not punishing you?

3. How did Jesus react to the disciples when he met them after the crucifixion and they didn't even recognize him?

Luke 15:11-24

1. As you read this, look for how the younger son wronged his father and how the father reacted to his son.

2. What drove the son back home?

3. What was the son's attitude when he returned to his father?

4. Even though it was highly unusual for the younger son to ask for his share of the inheritance, the father gave the son money and freedom. Do you think he was wise to do so? Is God any different with us?

[11]Jesus continued: "There was a man who had two sons. [12]The younger one said to his father, 'Father, give me my share of the estate.' So he divided his property between them.

[13]"Not long after that, the younger son got together all he had, set off for a distant country and there squandered his wealth in wild living. [14]After he had spent everything, there was a severe famine in that whole country, and he began to be in need. [15]So he went and hired himself out to a citizen of that country, who sent him to his fields to feed pigs. [16]He longed to fill his stomach with the pods that the pigs were eating, but no one gave him anything.

[17]"When he came to his senses, he said, 'How many of my father's hired men have food to spare, and here I am starving to death! [18]I will set out and go back to my father and say to him: Father, I have sinned against heaven and against you. [19]I am no longer worthy to be called your son; make me like one of your hired men.' [20]So he got up and went to his father.

"But while he was still a long way off, his father saw him and was filled with compassion for him; he ran to his son, threw his arms around him and kissed him.

[21]"The son said to him, 'Father, I have sinned against heaven and against you. I am no longer worthy to be called your son.'

[22]"But the father said to his servants, 'Quick! Bring the best robe and put it on him. Put a ring on his finger and sandals on his feet. [23] Bring the fattened calf and kill it. Let's have a feast and celebrate. [24]For this son of mine was dead and is alive again; he was lost and is found.' So they began to celebrate."

5. Can you identify with the younger son? At this point in your life, do you think you are more like him at the beginning of the story when he asked for his inheritance, or in the middle when he was in a faraway place living it up, or at the end when he came to his senses and asked for his father's forgiveness?

6. How does this story affect your idea of what God is like? How will it help you approach God?

Group Talk

1. What did you write for the first Warm-up question about meeting Jesus? Discuss it with the group.
2. What's the best way for God to help people come to their senses?
3. What should be our attitude toward those who seem to be too busy living on the edge to pay attention to God?

7 PARABLES: JESUS THE STORYTELLER

START HERE →

Persistence Pays Off

Harry was a happy-go-lucky kind of guy. He was pretty easy to get along with too. If you wanted to go to the game, Harry was in. If you'd decided you'd rather stay home and shoot pool, Harry was OK with that too. He didn't care much about stuff either—anything his mother picked out for him to wear was fine with Harry. But there was one thing Harry wanted. Badly.

Harry wanted a dog. A big dog to horse around with. Harry loved dogs. Problem was, Harry's father hated dogs. Whenever he asked his folks if he could get a dog, Harry's dad said, "No way." No matter how much Harry promised to take care of the dog himself, no matter how much he begged and whined, the answer was always, "No way." But Harry wouldn't give up.

Every single night at the dinner table, he'd ask again. "How about it, Dad?"

Harry's folks got pretty sick of listening to Harry. On the ninety-sixth night of this routine, Harry asked his usual question. "Could I please, please, puh-leeze get a dog?"

"Yes," said his dad. "You can get a dog." He knew he'd go nuts if he ever had to listen to Harry ask that question again. So he finally gave in and said yes.

Persistence. It paid off for Harry. And it pays off for us. After all, the stuff we really care about—stuff like getting an 'A' in geometry, making the varsity soccer team, landing a part in the school play—takes a bit of effort.

Jesus told his disciples a story about a persistent woman. She got results because she kept on asking for what she wanted. In the same way, says Jesus, we ought to keep on praying and never give up.

I'm not saying that God eventually says yes to every request we have. Sometimes God flat-out says no; other times God doesn't seem to be listening, and we don't get an answer. But remember that God knows your heart. God knows (better than you know) what's best for you. So keep on praying. Don't give up. You can bet God will answer your prayers.

1. What have you accomplished so far that you are most proud of?

2. What characteristics do you look for in a best friend?
   ___funny
   ___kind
   ___good-looking
   ___loyal
   ___silly
   ___a good listener
   ___fan of the Toronto Maple Leafs
   ___likes to spend time with you
   ___other: _____

3. What are some of the reasons God wants to talk with us on a daily basis?

Luke 18:1-8

1. As you read this, look for the technique the widow used to get her way.

2. Describe the judge in this story. Describe God.

3. What was the widow asking the judge for? Was this a legitimate request?

[1]Then Jesus told his disciples a parable to show them that they should always pray and not give up. [2]He said: "In a certain town there was a judge who neither feared God nor cared about men. [3]And there was a widow in that town who kept coming to him with the plea, 'Grant me justice against my adversary.'

[4]"For some time he refused. But finally he said to himself, 'Even though I don't fear God or care about men, [5]yet because this widow keeps bothering me, I will see that she gets justice, so that she won't eventually wear me out with her coming!'"

[6]And the Lord said, "Listen to what the unjust judge says. [7]And will not God bring about justice for his chosen ones, who cry out to him day and night? Will he keep putting them off? [8]I tell you, he will see that they get justice, and quickly. However, when the Son of Man comes, will he find faith on the earth?"

4. Does persistence in prayer mean repetitious or boring prayers? What does it mean to pray persistently?

5. What was the widow's attitude toward the judge? Do we need to have the same attitude toward God?

6. How will you put what you've learned about persistent prayer into practice this week?

Group Talk

1. Have you prayed for years for something? What kinds of things should you make a daily matter of prayer?

2. What can we learn from doing something on a daily basis?

3. How do you know God is listening to your prayers when you don't get an answer for a very long time?

PROVERBS: GREAT ADVICE FOR EVERYDAY LIVING

START HERE →

warmUP

Choosing the Right Lens

We live in the information age. We're bombarded with information, more than we ever wanted to know. Used to be, when you needed some information for a school research paper, you'd get yourself over to the library, grab a couple of books from the shelf, and find the sections that would help you learn about your topic. Now you just fire up your search engine, type in a keyword, and you'll find hundreds of entries—so many that narrowing it down is itself a huge job.

There's more. If you're a warm body, you're the focus of all kinds of ads and commercials telling you what you should be and how you should look. (Even if you hardly ever watch TV or go to movies.) Popular culture—films, books, magazines, radio, TV—sets the standard for how we should dress, think, and act. Of course all this information comes free of charge.

On top of that, we spend our lives going to school and church and youth groups and music lessons and teams of all sorts where we get filled up with other kinds of information. In the end, however, it's not so much what you know, but how you interpret what you know and how you act on it—the wisdom you show—that's important. As someone once said, "Wisdom is not just acquired information, but practical insight with spiritual implications."

This section focuses on the book of Proverbs. It's a book Solomon, Israel's wisest king, either wrote or had compiled. What's it all about? Practical living. Proverbs guides us in making the everyday decisions we face at work, in our families, with our friends, or at school.

According to Solomon, what is at the very center of wisdom? Fearing God. Trying to live according to God's will. Let's find out what this looks like.

1. Here are some modern proverbs you may have heard. What does each mean?
   a. Too many cooks spoil the stew.
   b. A watched pot never boils.
   c. The early bird catches the worm.
   d. Haste makes waste.
   e. Those who sleep with puppies wake up with fleas.
   f. (Add your favorite to the list!)

2. What's the difference between "book smarts" and "street smarts"? Which would you rather have?

3. The disciple Peter was a pretty impulsive guy. But he was also the guy whom Jesus nicknamed "Rock" and on whom Jesus built his church. Think of some times when he showed wisdom. Then list some foolish moves on his part.

proverbs 1:1–7

1. As you read these two sentences, decide which sentence is the introduction and which is the theme for the book.

2. What is the purpose of the book of Proverbs?

3. Who was Proverbs written for?

¹The proverbs of Solomon son of David, king of Israel:
²for attaining wisdom and discipline;
        for understanding words of insight;
³for acquiring a disciplined and prudent life,
        doing what is right and just and fair;
⁴for giving prudence to the simple,
        knowledge and discretion to the young—
⁵let the wise listen and add to their learning,
        and let the discerning get guidance—
⁶for understanding proverbs and parables,
        the sayings and riddles of the wise.
⁷The fear of the LORD is the beginning of knowledge,
        but fools despise wisdom and discipline.

4. "The fear of the LORD is the beginning of wisdom" (v. 7). What other gods do people try to live by?

5. The author says flat-out that "fools despise wisdom" (v. 7). What do you think makes foolish people act the way they do? What are the consequences of their actions?

6. How will you apply what you've learned in this passage to a specific situation you are dealing with?

Group Talk

1. Do we get mostly information (knowledge) in church or mostly wisdom? What, if anything, do knowledge and wisdom have to do with each other?
2. Think of someone who seems very wise to you. What characteristics does this person have? How does he or she show wisdom?
3. Is wisdom an important quality for our political leaders? Make up a campaign ad that focuses on wisdom for a politician who is running for president or another political office.

START HERE →

warmUP

Wisdom Is Calling

Last time, we learned that the fear of the Lord is the beginning of wisdom. That we should examine life by the rules made by the Creator God. That if we do so, we'll have a good life (but not necessarily one that is easy or free of suffering).

What are the effects of not listening to wisdom? In a word, not good.

If you're listening for it, wisdom isn't so hard to hear. In fact, Proverbs tells us that wisdom makes sure she is heard by standing at the corners of busy main streets, urging us to do what is right. The opposite of wisdom, folly, usually whispers her destructive advice in secret.

Generally speaking, there's a big difference between doing what's right and doing what's wrong. Certainly, some decisions are more difficult than others. Sometimes doing what's right falls into a gray area where there are a number of right things to choose from. Should you apply to this school or that one? Major in art or business? Try out for the soccer team or the improv team? No matter what we need to decide, wisdom speaks to us from many sources—teachers, parents, youth group leaders, friends, pastors.

Folly is choosing not to accept wisdom's advice. When you choose folly over wisdom, disaster results! Don't expect to lie to your folks about where you've been and still be able to enjoy their trust. Don't expect to sleep with your boyfriend/girlfriend and not get hurt. Don't expect to skip classes and neglect your homework and get good grades and a scholarship. Disaster, distress, and trouble are the fruit of folly, says the writer of Proverbs. A painful lesson most of us have learned.

Here's the deal: when we act with wisdom, God gives us more wisdom. When we choose to ignore God and act like fools, God allows us to experience the consequences of our actions. So go out and listen to the clear voice of wisdom. Ignore the siren song of folly. It's a no-brainer.

1. What was the good advice that the following people received but chose to ignore?
   a. Cinderella
   b. Lot's wife (see Gen. 19:17, 26)
   c. Darva Conger (of *Who Wants to Marry A Millionaire* fame)
   d. fill in your own example

2. Who was the last person who gave you good advice that you wish you had taken?
   ___coach
   ___friend
   ___parent
   ___other: _____

3. Why do you think it's so hard to take advice from others?

proverbs 1:20-33

1. As you read this, look for the results of refusing wisdom and of accepting wisdom.

2. How difficult is it to hear the voice of wisdom? Where can one go to hear wisdom?

3. How does wisdom react when she is ignored repeatedly?

²⁰Wisdom calls aloud in the street,
    she raises her voice in the public squares;
²¹at the head of the noisy streets she cries out,
    in the gateways of the city she makes her speech:
²²"How long will you simple ones love your simple ways?
    How long will mockers delight in mockery
    and fools hate knowledge?
²³If you had responded to my rebuke,
    I would have poured out my heart to you
    and made my thoughts known to you.
²⁴But since you rejected me when I called
    and no one gave heed when I stretched out my hand,
²⁵since you ignored all my advice
    and would not accept my rebuke,
²⁶I in turn will laugh at your disaster;
    I will mock when calamity overtakes you—
²⁷when calamity overtakes you like a storm,
    when disaster sweeps over you like a whirlwind,
    when distress and trouble overwhelm you.
²⁸"Then they will call to me but I will not answer;
    they will look for me but will not find me.
²⁹Since they hated knowledge
    and did not choose to fear the LORD,
³⁰since they would not accept my advice
    and spurned my rebuke,
³¹they will eat the fruit of their ways
    and be filled with the fruit of their schemes.
³²For the waywardness of the simple will kill them,
    and the complacency of fools will destroy them;
³³but whoever listens to me will live in safety
    and be at ease, without fear of harm."

4. What are the sources of wisdom in your life?

___parents
___magazines
___teachers
___friends
___the Bible/God
___movies
___other: _____

What stops you from listening more closely to wisdom?

5. Think of a foolish decision you made. Did you make a conscious choice between wisdom and folly? What were the consequences?

6. How will you apply what you learned from this lesson to a situation you are facing right now?

group Talk

1. Sometimes a friend won't listen to wisdom about poor behavior or unhealthy relationships. Is there anything you can do? What is your responsibility to that person?
2. "For the waywardness of the simple will kill them, and the complacency of fools will destroy them; but whoever listens to me will live ... without fear of harm" (vv. 32-33). Is this true in your experience? Why is it that foolish people sometimes seem to get ahead while those who listen to wisdom suffer?

PROVERBS: GREAT ADVICE FOR EVERYDAY LIVING

START HERE →

*warm*UP

Trust Me!

I've heard that Christianity is the easiest religion in the world because it costs nothing. On the other hand, people have also said that Christianity is the most difficult religion in the world because it costs everything. Which is correct?

The fact is, many people find Christianity far too costly. They just can't bring themselves to give their hearts to God. Why is that? Because they want to stay in control.

Proverbs puts it this way: "Lean not on your own understanding" (3:5). Don't rely on yourself, it says. Trust God instead. But that's easier said than done. We desperately want to call the shots. We have a hard time with anybody telling us what to do. Take Dave. He can't stand his parents anymore. "They're always telling me what to do," he complains. "They treat me like a little kid—they've got rules for everything." So Dave breaks 'em as fast as they make 'em. He stays away from home for days at a time. He smokes pot and drinks. He steals from his parents. He skips school. He's in control.

There's a little of Dave in all of us. We hate to have anybody telling us what to do. But control is exactly what God wants from us. Don't get me wrong. God's perfectly willing to let us call the shots ourselves. And to let us experience the consequences. But because God loves us, he offers this invitation: Trust me. Let me be in charge of your life.

If you're willing to trust God, you're in for an adventure. Once you let God sit in the driver's seat, who knows where you'll go?

1. What is the craziest thing you've ever done?

2. Which of the following activities have you tried (or would like to try)? Do you like doing things in which you have no control?
___ parasailing
___ mountain climbing
___ skydiving
___ bungee jumping
___ other: _____

3. Who tries to control your life? How do you feel about these people?

proverbs 3:5-10

⁵Trust in the LORD with all your heart
and lean not on your own understanding;
⁶in all your ways acknowledge him,
and he will make your paths straight.
⁷Do not be wise in your own eyes;
fear the LORD and shun evil.
⁸This will bring health to your body
and nourishment to your bones.
⁹Honor the LORD with your wealth,
with the firstfruits of all your crops;
¹⁰then your barns will be filled to overflowing,
and your vats will brim over with new wine.

1. As you read, look for what you must give to the Lord.

2. What parts of our lives does God want control of?

3. What are the benefits of submitting to God's control over our lives?

4. What part of this advice do you find easy to accept? What part is difficult? Why?

5. Why does God want complete control of our lives?

6. Are there areas of your life over which you are trying to maintain control? Explain why it's difficult to let go of control in these areas. Share some ideas about how to let God take control.

group Talk

1. What do you find encouraging and/or discouraging about this passage?
2. What does it mean to be "wise in your own eyes"? How can we avoid this pitfall?
3. What motivates you to bring God your "firstfruits"? What are your firstfruits?

START HERE ➞

warm UP

Discipline

You tiptoe in at 1:30 a.m. Avoid the third step—the one that squeaks. Grope your way along the hallway, past your parents' bedroom door. Attain the safety of your own room. Only to find your mom sitting on your bed. She's been waiting since midnight, and she's not happy. The excuses you've prepared sound lame, even to your own ears. She spits out the consequences. No car. Not for a month.

Discipline. A harsh word. It has to do with punishment and with making yourself do what you don't want to do. That may be true. But a lot depends on who's doing the discipline. If it's handed out by someone who doesn't care about you, you have good reason to fear. On the other hand, you can assume that the discipline handed out by your mom or your favorite teacher is going to do you good.

So it is with God's discipline. We've been talking about trusting God. Part of that trust is believing that God knows better than we do what's best for us. We may not know exactly what is going on in our lives or where we're headed. But the God who loves us is working to make us more like himself. And that involves correcting us when we go the opposite direction.

When things go wrong in our lives—things like getting sick, like broken relationships or failure or emotional pain—it's tough to know what is discipline and what is simply the natural consequence of sin. All the more reason to trust God. God knows what is going on. God knows what's best for us.

1. What is the most trouble you've ever been in?

2. What things do you do because they're good for you, even if you don't like to do them?
   ___ eat spinach
   ___ exercise
   ___ study for tests
   ___ floss your teeth
   ___ other: _____

3. What are some things God could use to make us better people (even if we don't find them pleasant)?

proverbs 3:11-12; 10:17; 13:18; 23:13

3:11 Do not despise the LORD's discipline
   and do not resent his rebuke,
12 because the LORD disciplines those he loves,
   as a father the son he delights in.

10:17 He who heeds discipline shows the way to life,
   but whoever ignores correction leads others astray.

13:18 He who ignores discipline comes to poverty and shame,
   but whoever heeds correction is honored.

23:13 Do not withhold discipline from a child;
   if you punish him with the rod, he will not die.

1. As you read this, list the consequences of not accepting discipline.

2. What other words are used for discipline in these passages?

3. What is the goal of discipline?

4. People who study the relationships between parents and their children have said that kids actually welcome discipline because it shows their parents care. Do you agree? Why or why not?

5. What kinds of problems might children have if their parents didn't bother to discipline them or disciplined them unfairly?

6. Think of an area in your life where you want to practice more self-discipline. Talk with the group about what you could do to be more disciplined in this area.

Group Talk

1. What makes it hard for us to accept discipline? (The passages from Proverbs assume we should want to be disciplined.) How can we become more accepting of discipline?
2. From whom is it easy to accept discipline? From whom do you have a hard time accepting discipline? How can you can learn to deal with this?
3. Is discipline always helpful? Explain.

warmUP

Consider the Ant

You've seen the bumper sticker: I'd Rather Be Fishing. Quick—what would you rather be doing right now? Fishing? Taking a nap? Climbing a mountain? Playing soccer? Painting a picture? Watching a movie? Dancing? Reading a novel? Great! The choices are limited only by your imagination. God wants us to enjoy this dazzling creation. He wants us to relax and have fun.

But our recreation has a purpose. It's to prepare us for work. That's right, work. There is work for each of us in God's kingdom. If we spend our lives simply trying to get by, doing as little as we possibly can, God has a name for us— "sluggard." And God is not pleased with sluggards.

Get down on your knees and watch an anthill for a while, says the writer of Proverbs. There's your example of how to work. The busy ants can be your source of wisdom. Fine, you say. That's the nature of ants. But why should *I* work hard?

Several reasons. For one thing, we represent Christ to others. So our reputation is the Lord's reputation in the minds of our neighbors. For another, working hard keeps us out of trouble. Spending our time diligently carrying out God's will in our lives keeps us from temptations. Finally, God knows what is best for us—if we decide not to follow God's direction for our lives, we're inviting disaster.

God's not a workaholic and doesn't want you to be one either. That's why God created the rhythm of work and play and rest. Enjoy them all!

1. What's your favorite form of recreation or relaxation?

2. What do you suppose God did on the seventh day of creation when he rested?
   ___ took a nap
   ___ went for a walk
   ___ went fishing
   ___ figured out what to do next
   ___ other:

3. Why do you work?
   ___ need money
   ___ like the job
   ___ something to do
   ___ to build my resumé
   ___ other: _____

Proverbs 6:6-11

1. As you read this, notice what the ant does that is so good.

2. What does laziness bring about?

3. Imagine Solomon saying these verses to someone who's lazy. Try reading the verses that way.

⁶Go to the ant, you sluggard;
          consider its ways and be wise!
⁷It has no commander,
          no overseer or ruler,
⁸yet it stores its provisions in summer
          and gathers its food at harvest.
⁹How long will you lie there, you sluggard?
          When will you get up from your sleep?
¹⁰A little sleep, a little slumber,
          a little folding of the hands to rest—
¹¹and poverty will come on you like a bandit
          and scarcity like an armed man.

4. Do you do your work without prompting, like the ant? In what ways are you like the sluggard?

5. Too much rest, says Proverbs, and "poverty will come on you like a bandit." Is poverty always the result of unwillingness to work hard? What other reasons cause poverty?

6. How could this passage affect your attitude toward work this coming week?

Group Talk

1. How can we tell the difference between what is rest and what is laziness? Share your ideas for developing a proper balance in your life between rest and work and play.
2. Is there such a thing as working too hard? What happens to people when they spend all their energy doing their work? Share examples you know of.
3. How do you deal with people who are lazy—at school or at work or in your family?

PROVERBS: GREAT ADVICE FOR EVERYDAY LIVING

START HERE →

*warm*UP

The Power of Words

God definitely created the passage of time with us in mind. When we do something great, like winning the state championship in volleyball, we can celebrate, but life goes on. We need to keep working and playing. Next year, it's more than likely someone else is going to take home that trophy. And when we feel like life couldn't possibly get any worse—we've lost our best friend or messed up a run during symphony tryouts—the passage of time can help us heal.

Every new second we live offers another opportunity to do right or to do wrong. And for no part of us is this truer than for our tongues. It only takes a second to build someone up ("What a great poem you wrote for English class!") or tear someone down ("You want a friend? Buy a hamster.").

Proverbs has lots to say about the words that come out of our mouths. Your words have power over other people. But maybe you don't realize that they also have power over you. When you build others up, you get built up as well. When you tear others down, it hurts you too. Like all sin, words can damage us. You are not like a computer that remains unchanged by its data.

Here's the good news: you can use the power of words to become more like the person God wants you to be. Because the more you lift up and encourage the people God puts in your life, the more you reflect God's image.

1. Describe your favorite commercial. What phrases or words stick with you?

2. Tell the group the best compliment you've ever received. Don't be shy!

3. Why did God make our tongues so versatile?

proverbs 26:20-26; proverbs 24:26

26:20 Without wood a fire goes out;
    without gossip a quarrel dies down.
21 As charcoal to embers and as wood to fire,
    so is a quarrelsome man for kindling strife.
22 The words of a gossip are like choice morsels;
    they go down to a man's inmost parts.
23 Like a coating of glaze over earthenware
    are fervent lips with an evil heart.
24 A malicious man disguises himself with his lips,
    but in his heart he harbors deceit.
25 Though his speech is charming, do not believe him,
    for seven abominations fill his heart.
26 His malice may be concealed by deception,
    but his wickedness will be exposed in the assembly.

24:26 An honest answer is like a kiss on the lips.

1. As you read this, look for the things words are compared to.

2. What are the best ways for stopping arguments?

3. Describe the malicious person.

4. How can we avoid the temptation to gossip about others? What could be your response when you are with people who are spreading gossip?

5. Proverbs 24:26 says, "An honest answer is like a kiss on the lips." Is honesty always the best policy? Can you think of a situation where honest words may be used to hurt people or tear them down rather than build them up?

6. How will this lesson affect the way you use words this week?

group Talk

1. If affirming people is so easy, why don't we do it more often? Share ideas for building people up this week.
2. Sometimes words slide out of our mouths before we've had time to think about them. When we're with our friends, we go for the quick laugh without stopping to consider if it's at someone else's expense. Share strategies to stop hurting people thoughtlessly.
3. How does technology intensify the power of our words? (Think e-mail and Internet chat rooms!)

7 PROVERBS: GREAT ADVICE FOR EVERYDAY LIVING

warm UP

Superwoman

The book of Proverbs has as its theme, "The fear of the Lord is the beginning of knowledge." It begins with the words of Lady Wisdom crying loudly in the streets; it ends with this portrait of the ideal woman whose life shows the practical everyday results of living according to "the fear of the Lord."

Now, for anyone who still believes that the ideal Christian woman is a shy, quiet, stay-behind-the-scenes soccer mom, this passage should be required reading. The "wife of noble character," as she is called, is some kind of Superwoman. She buys fields, she farms, she oversees business transactions, she sews all kinds of clothing. She takes care of her family, and the poor and helpless besides. She's amazing!

So what's the point here? you may be wondering. Isn't this woman some kind of unrealistic ideal, someone I could never hope to be like? No! The point is this: men and women who put God first are blessed. Their lives bear the generous fruit of the Holy Spirit's work—love, joy, peace, patience, kindness, goodness, faithfulness, gentleness, and self-control—and point to their Creator.

That's a mighty good reason for putting the "fear of the Lord" first in our lives. God will take care of the rest.

1. Who do you think most represents the ideal woman?
___ Mary Poppins
___ Princess Leia
___ Mother Teresa
___ Jael (see Judges 4:14-22)
___ other: _____

2. Name five strong women portrayed in popular culture—movies, TV shows, books, or music.
a. _____
b. _____
c. _____
d. _____
e. _____

3. What woman do you look up to most? What qualities do you like about her?

Proverbs 31:10-31

10 A wife of noble character who can find?
   She is worth far more than rubies.
11 Her husband has full confidence in her
   and lacks nothing of value.
12 She brings him good, not harm,
   all the days of her life.
13 She selects wool and flax
   and works with eager hands.
14 She is like the merchant ships,
   bringing her food from afar.
15 She gets up while it is still dark;
   she provides food for her family
   and portions for her servant girls.
16 She considers a field and buys it;
   out of her earnings she plants a vineyard.
17 She sets about her work vigorously;
   her arms are strong for her tasks.
18 She sees that her trading is profitable,
   and her lamp does not go out at night.
19 In her hand she holds the distaff
   and grasps the spindle with her fingers.
20 She opens her arms to the poor
   and extends her hands to the needy.
21 When it snows, she has no fear for her household;
   for all of them are clothed in scarlet.
22 She makes coverings for her bed;
   she is clothed in fine linen and purple.
23 Her husband is respected at the city gate,
   where he takes his seat among the elders of the land.
24 She makes linen garments and sells them,
   and supplies the merchants with sashes.
25 She is clothed with strength and dignity;
   she can laugh at the days to come.
26 She speaks with wisdom,
   and faithful instruction is on her tongue.
27 She watches over the affairs of her household
   and does not eat the bread of idleness.
28 Her children arise and call her blessed;
   her husband also, and he praises her:
29 "Many women do noble things,
   but you surpass them all."
30 Charm is deceptive, and beauty is fleeting;
   but a woman who fears the Lord is to be praised.
31 Give her the reward she has earned,
   and let her works bring her praise at the city gate.

1. As you read this passage, look for a physical description of this "wife of noble character."

2. Make a list of all her accomplishments.

3. What is the source of her accomplishments?

4. According to most TV programs and movies, what qualities does the ideal woman have? The ideal man? Does Proverbs 31 describe the same qualities?

5. No one person is really gifted to do all this. What should we learn from this list?

6. Guys, how would you describe the ideal high school woman? Girls, how would you describe the ideal high school man? Compare lists. Do your descriptions match what is considered the ideal at your school?

Group Talk

1. Many teenagers read fashion magazines like *Seventeen, YM, Mademoiselle,* and others. These magazines portray an image of women—and men too—that often contradicts the ideal of Proverbs 31. Is there anything wrong with reading these magazines? Why or why not?

2. There's a lot of talk these days about gender issues. Many women are capably doing jobs and filling leadership roles their grandmothers would not have had a chance to do. Have the ideals of feminism been achieved in your school, or is there still room for improvement when it comes to the roles that guys and girls fill?

1 PHILEMON: DOING THE RIGHT THING

START HERE →

warmUP

A Bold Request

Betrayal, escape, crimes worthy of death, and what to do about such stuff are the subjects of Paul's postcard-size letter to Philemon. It all begins like this: Philemon is a Christian who has a slave, Onesimus.

Maybe you're already thinking "Whoa! There's something wrong here. How could Philemon be a Christian *and* a slave owner? And why doesn't Paul let him have it with both barrels?"

Well, it's like this: Slavery was an accepted practice in the Roman Empire. Unlike American slavery, it was not based on race, nor was it always permanent; slaves could buy their way to freedom. Paul doesn't command slave owners like Philemon to set their slaves free because he knew there was no way slavery could end at that time—the Romans simply wouldn't allow it. So Paul writes to Philemon within this context.

Anyway, Onesimus escapes and comes into contact with the gospel. His world unravels. He meets Paul. They both agree that he needs to return to Philemon. So Paul writes this letter. And so begins the adventure.

Paul knew that, legally, Philemon could severely punish Onesimus for running away; in fact, he could even have Onesimus killed. So Paul crafts his letter carefully. He praises Philemon for his outstanding service to Christ and to others. Then Paul makes a bold request: take Onesimus back, he says. And then he goes one step further. Take him back as a brother in Christ!

Today we'll take a look at the first part of Paul's letter to Philemon.

1. Jesus didn't have much in this world—no house, car, stocks, savings accounts, high-power job. How do you suppose he lived?

2. What are the reasons we find it hard to ask people to do stuff for us?
   ___pride
   ___independence
   ___fear of rejection
   ___other: _____

3. When you approach your parents to make a huge request, what's your style?

Philemon 1-12

1. As you read, watch for the good things Paul says about Philemon.

2. What topics does Paul focus on in this letter?

3. What is Paul basing his appeal to Philemon on, since he's not going to order him to do the right thing?

[1]Paul, a prisoner of Christ Jesus, and Timothy our brother,

To Philemon our dear friend and fellow worker, [2]to Apphia our sister, to Archippus our fellow soldier and to the church that meets in your home:

[3]Grace to you and peace from God our Father and the Lord Jesus Christ.

[4]I always thank my God as I remember you in my prayers, [5]because I hear about your faith in the Lord Jesus and your love for all the saints. [6]I pray that you may be active in sharing your faith, so that you will have a full understanding of every good thing we have in Christ. [7]Your love has given me great joy and encouragement, because you, brother, have refreshed the hearts of the saints.

[8]Therefore, although in Christ I could be bold and order you to do what you ought to do, [9]yet I appeal to you on the basis of love. I then, as Paul—an old man and now also a prisoner of Christ Jesus—[10]I appeal to you for my son Onesimus, who became my son while I was in chains. [11]Formerly he was useless to you, but now he has become useful both to you and to me.

[12]I am sending him—who is my very heart—back to you.

4. Could Paul be accused of "buttering up" Philemon so he'll feel guilty if he doesn't take Onesimus back?

5. "Formerly he [Onesimus] was useless to you," says Paul, "but now he has become useful both to you and to me." What does Paul mean? What caused the change?

6. Do you relate more to Onesimus, Philemon, or Paul? What lessons for your own life will you take from this letter?

Group Talk

1. Do we need to send and receive more letters of encouragement to walk in the Christian faith? What difference might such letters make in our everyday ability to do the right thing?
2. Do you usually respond better if someone makes you do something or if they ask you to do it of your own free will?
3. Paul assumes that Philemon will do the right thing and receive Onesimus with open arms as a brother in Christ. What might happen to Onesimus's faith if Philemon treats him harshly? How does the way we treat others reflect on our walk with Christ?

PHILEMON: DOING THE RIGHT THING

START HERE ⟶

*warm*UP

A Better Way

When last we left Paul, he was thanking Philemon for being a Christian brother who lived out his faith. Now Paul asks Philemon to continue to do so by taking back his runaway slave Onesimus. Not only that, Paul asks Philemon not to punish Onesimus but instead to embrace him back into the family. Paul does this for two reasons.

First, Onesimus has become a Christian. Although Paul never states it in this letter, he believes that in Christ, slavery should not exist (Gal. 3:28). Onesimus should be set free; he should serve Philemon of his own free will, not because he is a slave. Paul wants to suggest a better working arrangement between the two.

Second, Paul is undoubtedly worried about Philemon as well. Although Onesimus is the slave, Paul knows that if Philemon stays angry at Onesimus, bitter about the way he, Philemon, has been treated, he himself will be enslaved. Forgiving needs be a way of life for everyone—not only for the sake of those we forgive, but for our own sake as well. Doing the right thing is a win-win situation!

1. What's the most fun/craziest thing you've ever done for your friends? What's the craziest thing your friends have ever done for you?

2. Think of a time when you needed to ask forgiveness from a fellow Christian—maybe your parents or a teacher or a friend. Was it difficult to do? How did they respond?

3. What were some of the things the disciples did for which Jesus forgave them?

Philemon 13-25

1. As you read this, look for the reasons Paul uses to convince Philemon to forgive Onesimus.

2. Paul seems to need Onesimus. Why does he send him back?

3. What is Paul willing to accept on behalf of Onesimus?

[13]I would have liked to keep him with me so that he could take your place in helping me while I am in chains for the gospel. [14]But I did not want to do anything without your consent, so that any favor you do will be spontaneous and not forced. [15]Perhaps the reason he was separated from you for a little while was that you might have him back for good—[16]no longer as a slave, but better than a slave, as a dear brother. He is very dear to me but even dearer to you, both as a man and as a brother in the Lord.

[17]So if you consider me a partner, welcome him as you would welcome me. [18]If he has done you any wrong or owes you anything, charge it to me. [19]I, Paul, am writing this with my own hand. I will pay it back—not to mention that you owe me your very self. [20]I do wish, brother, that I may have some benefit from you in the Lord; refresh my heart in Christ. [21]Confident of your obedience, I write to you, knowing that you will do even more than I ask. [22]And one thing more: Prepare a guest room for me, because I hope to be restored to you in answer to your prayers.

[23]Epaphras, my fellow prisoner in Christ Jesus, sends you greetings. [24]And so do Mark, Aristarchus, Demas and Luke, my fellow workers.

[25]The grace of the Lord Jesus Christ be with your spirit.

4. When should you forgive someone?

___when he or she asks
___when the act is committed
___when he or she acts sorry
___when you feel like it
___other: _____

5. Paul expects the best from Philemon. What should you expect from other Christians when you ask for something?

6. What does this passage teach about forgiveness? How will you apply this to your own life this week?

Group Talk

1. How does not forgiving others limit and enslave us?
2. Do others see Christ in your life? What can block that from happening? Discuss ways of overcoming these obstacles.